The
Quotable
Woman

The Quotable Woman

Words of Wisdom
from Mother Teresa, Edith Wharton,
Virginia Woolf, Eleanor Roosevelt,
Katharine Hepburn, and More

CAROL A. TURKINGTON

McGraw-Hill

New York   San Francisco   Washington, D.C.   Auckland   Bogotá
Caracas   Lisbon   London   Madrid   Mexico City   Milan
Montreal   New Delhi   San Juan   Singapore
Sydney   Tokyo   Toronto

McGraw-Hill

A Division of The **McGraw·Hill** Companies

This book was set in Berkeley by North Market Street Graphics.

Printed and bound by R. R. Donnelley & Sons Company.

McGraw-Hill books are available at special quantity discounts to use as premiums and sales promotions, or for use in corporate training programs. For more information, please write to the Director of Special Sales, Professional Publishing, McGraw-Hill, Two Penn Plaza, New York, NY 10121-2298. Or contact your local bookstore.

This publication is designed to provide accurate and authoritative information in regard to the subject matter covered. It is sold with the understanding that neither the author nor the publisher is engaged in rendering legal, accounting, or other professional service. If legal advice or other expert assistance is required, the services of a competent professional person should be sought.
—From a Declaration of Principles jointly adopted by a Committee of the American Bar Association and a Committee of Publishers.

# Dedication

A little while when I am gone
My life will live in music after me,
As spun foam lifted and borne on
After the wave is lost in the full sea.
—SARA TEASDALE

For Constance Dalmas Ruch (1911–2000),
for showing me the way

Contents

# Introduction

If neither governesses or mothers know, how can they teach? So
long as education is not provided for them, how can it be provided
by them?
— SARAH EMILY DAVIES (1860–1908), *Thoughts on Some Questions
Relating to Women*

Throughout the centuries, women have always had something to
say—even when no one was listening. But if women are to pass on
the knowledge we've learned from our mothers, and our mothers'
mothers, we must be able to hear their observations and their passions in their own words. Otherwise, how can we truly pass on
their thoughts to those women who come after us? If we are not
taught their wisdom, how can we pass on the legacy of their experience?

All too often, volumes of quotable quotes have focused on men.
From statesmen to shamans, philosophers to politicians, all have
been able to record their point of view. Women's wisdom is no less
profound for being so often ignored. This is why I wanted to write
The Quotable Woman.

Whether you're a speechwriter looking for that perfect quote, a
teacher hoping to inspire your students, or a trivia buff locked in a
dispute over who said what, *The Quotable Woman* brings together a
collection of viewpoints and observations from some of the most
fascinating and diverse women of all time. I've tried hard to include
not just the wealthy and the well-educated European white women
of the twentieth century, but haunting observations by women
from all walks of life, from many different lands and many centuries—Maya Angelou to Mae West, Sojourner Truth to Simone de
Beauvoir, Elizabeth I to Lady Murasaki.

The book is organized into dozens of thematic sections such as
"Anger," "Children," "Education," "Love," and "Politics," to make it

easy to find just the quote you're looking for on any particular topic. (If you're looking for quotes from a particular woman, you can turn to the index.)

Why a quote book? As I. E. Landon says in *Romance and Reality* (1831), "An apt quotation is like a lamp which flings its light over the whole sentence." Whether you're looking for a witty anecdote or taking solace in the wisdom of a kindred spirit, odds are you'll find it in the illuminating words of wise women such as Willa Cather, Golda Meir, Millicent Fenwick, Madeleine L'Engle, or Nadia Boulanger.

Any why? Because a good quotation or an illuminating idea can change your feelings, your outlook, and even your concept of life itself. As Emily Brontë wrote in *Wuthering Heights* (1847): "I've dreamt in my life dreams that have stayed with me ever after, and changed my ideas: they've gone through and through me, like wine through water, and altered the colour of my mind."

Carol Turkington

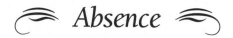# Absence

The heart may think it knows better; the senses know that absence blots people out. We have really no absent friends.
— ELIZABETH BOWEN, *The Death of the Heart,* 1966

When my self is not with you, it is nowhere.
— HÉLOÏSE, c. 1098–1164, letter to Peter Abelard

Moonlight, a wood fire, my own good lamp. What can I complain about? Only the absence of those I love.
— COLETTE, letter, January 3, 1928

My life will be sour grapes and ashes without you.
— DAISY ASHFORD, *The Young Visitors,* 1919

Absence becomes the greatest Presence.
— MAY SARTON, "Difficult Scene," *The Lion and the Rose,* 1948

Absence on Love effects the same
As winds oppos'd to fire
Extinguishes a feeble Flame
And blows a great one higher
— ANNE FINCH, "On Absence," *Miscellany Poems, written by a Lady,* 1713

It takes time for the absent to assume their true shape in our thoughts.
— COLETTE, *Sido,* 1929

(*See also* Alone, Farewell, Parting)

Activism

It is so much easier sometimes to sit down and be resigned than to rise up and be indignant.
— ELLA WINTER, *And Not to Yield*, 1963

The role of the Do-Gooder is not what actors call a fat part.
— MARGARET HALSEY, *The Folks at Home*, 1952

As citizens, we must prevent wrongdoing because the world in which we all live, wrong-doer, wrong-sufferer and spectator, is at stake.
— HANNAH ARENDT, *The Life of the Mind*, 1978

A small group of thoughtful people could change the world. Indeed, it's the only thing that ever has.
— MARGARET MEAD, *The Utne Reader*, 1992

There should be less talk . . . What do you do then? Take a broom and clean someone's house. That says enough.
— MOTHER TERESA, *A Gift for God*, 1975

Adolescence

At 14, you don't need sickness or death for tragedy.
— JESSAMYN WEST, *Cress Delahanty*, 1948

Show Miss Manners a grownup who has happy memories of teenage years, with their endless round of merry-making and dancing the night away, and Miss Manners will show you a person who has either no heart or no memory.
— JUDITH MARTIN, *Miss Manners' Guide to Rearing Perfect Children*, 1984

The invention of the teenager was a mistake. Once you identify a period of life in which people get to stay out late but don't have to pay taxes—naturally, nobody wants to live any other way.

— JUDITH MARTIN, *Miss Manner's Guide to Excruciatingly Correct Behavior,* 1982

Adolescence is just one big walking pimple.

— CAROL BURNETT, Phil Donahue show, NBC-TV, October 16, 1986

 *Adulthood*

Another belief of mine: that everyone else my age is an adult, whereas I am merely in disguise.

— MARGARET ATWOOD, *Cat's Eye,* 1988

Every human being on this earth is born with a tragedy . . . he's born with the tragedy that he has to grow up. He has lost everything that is lovely and must fight for a new loveliness of his own making, and it's a tragedy. A lot of people don't have the courage to do it.

— HELEN HAYES, in Roy Newquist's *Showcase,* 1966

Maybe I'm an adult because my friends are. Could that be the way you tell? My friends are tall and drink coffee and have sex. . . . Maybe no one actually turns into an adult. Maybe you just get to be an older and older kid. Maybe the whole world is being run by old kids.

— ADAIR LARA, *Welcome to Earth, Mom,* 1992

Was I the only woman in the world who, at my age—and after a lifetime of quite rampant independence—still did not quite feel grown up?

— DODIE SMITH, *The Town in Bloom,* 1965

We thought we were running away from the grownups, and now we are the grownups.

— MARGARET ATWOOD, *Cat's Eye,* 1988

Adventure

He's going for the adventure of it. They always have, no matter what excuse they've given, from the Holy Grail to the California gold fields. The difference in America is that the women have always gone along.

— EDNA FERBER, *Cimarron,* 1930

Nobody is ever met at the airport when beginning a new adventure. It's just not done.

— ELIZABETH WARNOCK FERNEA, *A View of the Nile,* 1970

God made the world round so we could never see too far down the road.

— ISAK DINESEN, recalled on her death, September 7, 1962

(*See also* Risk)

Adversity

One likes people much better when they're battered down by a prodigious siege of misfortune than when they triumph.

— VIRGINIA WOOLF, *A Writer's Diary,* edited by Leonard Woolf, 1954

When my enemies stop hissing, I shall know I'm slipping.

— MARIA CALLAS, in *Maria Callas,* 1981

It is not in the still calm of life . . . that great characters are formed. Great necessities call out great virtues.

— ABIGAIL ADAMS, letter to John Quincy Adams, January 19, 1780

It is not given to everyone to shine in adversity.

— JANE AIKEN HODGE, *Marry in Haste,* 1961

People are like stained-glass windows. They sparkle and shine when the sun is out, but when the darkness sets in, their true beauty is revealed only if there is a light from within.

— ELISABETH KÜBLER-ROSS, *To Live Until We Say Goodbye,* 1978

They sicken of the calm, who knew the storm.

— DOROTHY PARKER, *Fair Weather,* 1928

A strong hatred is the best lamp to bear in our hands as we go over the dark places of life, cutting away the dead things men tell us to revere.

— REBECCA WEST, *The Young Rebecca: Writings of Rebecca West 1911–17,* Jane Marcus (ed), 1981

If we had no winter, the spring would not be so pleasant; if we did not sometime taste of adversity, prosperity would not be so welcome.

— ANNE BRADSTREET, *Meditations Divine and Moral,* 1664

A clay pot sitting in the sun will always be a clay pot. It has to go through the white heat of the furnace to become porcelain.

— MILDRED WITTE STRUVEN, quoted by her daughter Jean Harris, *Stranger in Two Worlds,* 1986

(*See also* Problems)

Advertising

In this business, you can never wash the dinner dishes and say they are done. You have to keep doing them constantly.

— MARY WELLS LAWRENCE, on need for fresh approaches, *Time,* October 3, 1966

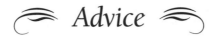

Advice

I give myself sometimes admirable advice, but I am incapable of taking it.
— LADY MARY WORTLEY MONTAGU, letter, 1725

"Pull yourself together" is seldom said to anyone who can.
— MIGNON MCLAUGHLIN, *The Neurotic's Notebook*, 1963

Advice is what we ask for when we already know the answer, but wish we didn't.
— ERICA JONG, *How to Save Your Own Life*, 1977

Advice is one of those things it is far more blessed to give than to receive.
— CAROLYN WELLS, *The Rest of My Life*, 1937

A woman in love never takes advice.
— ROSAMOND MARSHALL, *Kitty*, 1943

He had polyester sheets and I wanted to get cotton sheets. He discussed it with his shrink many times before he made the switch.
— MIA FARROW, of the dependence of her former partner, Woody Allen, on psychotherapists, *Independent*, February 8, 1997

Please give me some advice in your next letter. I promise not to follow it.
— EDNA ST. VINCENT MILLAY, as an undergraduate at Vassar, in Allen Ross Macdougall (ed), *Letters of Edna St. Vincent Millay*, 1952

Aerobics

Contrary to popular . . . opinion, aerobics have absolutely nothing to do with squeezing our body into hideous shiny Spandex, grinning like a deranged orangutan, and doing cretinous dance steps to debauched disco music.

— CYNTHIA HEIMEL, *Sex Tips for Girls*, 1983

Affairs

Adultery is a meanness and a stealing, a taking away from someone what should be theirs, a great selfishness, and surrounded and guarded by lies lest it should be found out. And out of the meanness and selfishness and lying flow love and joy and peace beyond anything that can be imagined.

— ROSE MACAULAY, *The Towers of Trebizond*, 1956

People who are so dreadfully devoted to their wives are so apt, from mere habit, to get devoted to other people's wives as well.

— JANE CARLYLE (1801), in Michele Brown and Ann O'Connor, Hammer and Tongues, 1986

There is nothing better for the spirit or body than a love affair. It elevates thoughts and flattens stomachs.

— BARBARA HOWARD, *Laughing All the Way*, 1973

No adultery is bloodless.

— NATALIE GINZBURG, *The City and the House*, 1985

I say I don't sleep with married men, but what I mean is that I don't sleep with happily married men.

— BRITT EKLAND, attributed, 1980, in Anne Stibbs (ed) *Like a Fish Needs a Bicycle,* 1992

If you bed people of below-stairs class, they will go to the papers.

— JANE CLARK, *Daily Telegraph,* May 31, 1994

(*See also* Falling in Love, First Love, Free Love, Love, Love Letters, Loving, Mature Love, May-December Romance, Memories of Love, True Love)

Affection

One is apt to think of people's affection as a fixed quantity, instead of a sort of moving sea with tide always going out or coming in, but still fundamentally there.

— FREYA STARK, *The Coast of Incense,* 1953

Trust in my affection for you. Tho' I may not display it exactly in the way you like and expect it, it is not therefore less deep and sincere.

— ANNA JAMESON (1833), in G. H. Needler, *Letters of Anna Jameson to Ottilie Von Goethe,* 1939

(*See also* Emotions, Falling in Love, First Love, Love, Love Letters, Love Versus Like, Loving, Mature Love, May-December Romance, Memories of Love, True Love)

Age

In a dream, you are never eighty.
— ANNE SEXTON, "Old," *All My Pretty Ones,* 1961

This is what 40 looks like. We've been lying for so long, who would know?
— GLORIA STEINEM, response when complimented by a reporter on not looking 40, quoted by Lisa Jardine in the *Sunday Times,* May 15, 1994

I used to think that getting old was about vanity—but actually it's about losing people you love.
— JOYCE CAROL OATES, in *The Guardian,* August 18, 1989

One day, there's a hand that goes over the face and changes it. You look like an apple that isn't young anymore.
— GRETA GARBO, in *Vanity Fair,* February 1994

At 50, you have the choice of keeping your face or your figure and it's much better to keep your face.
— DAME BARBARA CARTLAND, in *The Daily Mail,* July 10, 1981

It is a mistake to regard age as a downhill grade toward dissolution. The reverse is true. As one grows older, one climbs with surprising strides.
— GEORGE SAND, in Marie Jenny Howe (ed), *The Intimate Journal of George Sand,* 1929

The great thing about getting older is that you don't lose all the other ages you've been.
— MADELEINE L'ENGLE, *The New York Times,* 1985

The last steps of life are ever slow and difficult.
— MADAME DE STAEL, *Corinne,* 1807

To grow old is to have taken away, one by one, all gifts of life, the food and wine, the music and the company. . . . The gods unloose, one by one, the mortal fingers that cling to the edge of the table.
— STORM JAMESON, *Three Kingdoms*, 1926

Just as you begin to feel that you could make good use of time, there was no time left to you.
— LISA ALTHER, *Kinflicks*, 1975

I suppose real old age begins when one looks backward rather than forward.
— MAY SARTON, *At Seventy*, 1984

She was an old woman now, and her life had become memories.
— LESLIE MARMON SILKO, "Lullaby," *Storyteller*, 1981

There is no such thing as old age; there is only sorrow.
— EDITH WHARTON, *A Backward Glance*, 1934

How short the road has suddenly become,
The end of which seemed out of sight before!
— ANNA AKHMATOVA, "Why Wonder?" in *Poems*, 1988

If grass can grow through cement, love can find you at every time in your life.
— CHER, *The Times*, May 30, 1998

I gave my beauty and my youth to men. I am going to give my wisdom and experience to animals.
— BRIGITTE BARDOT, attributed, June 1987

The crucial task of old age is balance: keeping just well enough, just brave enough, just gay and interested and starkly honest enough to remain a sentient human being.
— FLORIDA SCOTT-MAXWELL, *The Measure of My Days*, 1968

I have everything I had 20 years ago, except now it's all lower.
— GYPSY ROSE LEE, *Newsweek,* September 16, 1968

How unnatural the imposed view, imposed by a puritanical ethos, that passionate love belongs only to the young, that people are dead from the neck down by the time they are forty, and that any deep feeling, any passion after that age, is either ludicrous or revolting.
— MAY SARTON, *Journal of a Solitude,* 1973

(*See also* Adulthood, Mature Love, Memories, Retirement)

Alcohol

Liquor is such a nice substitute for facing adult life.
— DOROTHY B. HUGHES, *In a Lonely Place,* 1947

Even though a number of people have tried, no one has yet found a way to drink for a living.
— JEAN KERR, *Poor Richard,* 1964

The true alcoholic takes the first drink for the person or situation or insult that upsets him. He takes the rest of the drinks for himself.
— LILLIAN ROTH, with Mike Connolly and Gerold Frank, *I'll Cry Tomorrow,* 1954

Alcoholism isn't a spectator sport. Eventually, the whole family gets to play.
— JOYCE ROBERTA-BURDITT, *The Cracker Factory,* 1977

Alcohol removes inhibitions, like that scared little mouse who got drunk and shook his whiskers and shouted: "Now bring on the damn cat!"
— ELEANOR EARLY, news summaries, January 30, 1950

(*See also* Drinking, Wine)

Alone

When you live alone, you can be sure that the person who squeezed the toothpaste tube in the middle wasn't committing a hostile act.
— ELLEN GOODMAN, *Close to Home,* 1979

Once you have lived with another, it is a great torture to have to live alone.
— CARSON MCCULLERS, *The Ballad of the Sad Cafe,* 1953

Anything we fully do is an alone journey.
— NATALIE GOLDBERG, *Writing Down the Bones,* 1986

When love is out of your life, you're through in a way. Because while it is there it's like a motor that's going, you have such vitality to do things, big things, because love is goosing you all the time.
— FANNY BRICE, in *The Fabulous Fanny,* by Norman Katkov, 1952

A woman without a man cannot meet a man, any man, of any age, without thinking, even if it's for a half-second, "Perhaps this is the man."
— DORIS LESSING, *The Golden Notebook,* 1962

Life alone can sink into a numbing sameness, punctuated only by whether or not the cat has thrown up on the rug today.
— BARBARA HOLLAND, *One's Company,* 1992

When I'm alone, I can sleep crossways in bed without an argument.
— ZSA ZSA GABOR, on being between marriages, *Family Weekly,* May 7, 1976

(*See also* Absence, Farewell, Loneliness, Parting, Solitude)

Alzheimer's Disease

She was losing her mind in handfuls.
> ━ MARION ROACH, on her mother, a victim of Alzheimer's disease, *Another Name for Madness*, 1985

(*See also* Age, Memories)

Ancestors

It isn't where you came from; it's where you're going that counts.
> ━ ELLA FITZGERALD, in *Ella Fitzgerald*, by Stuart Nicholson, 1994

Angels

Imagine them as they were first conceived
part musical instrument and part daisy
> ━ P. K. PAGE, "Images of Angels," *The Metal and the Flower*, 1954

Anger

Anger makes dull men witty, but it keeps them poor.
> ━ QUEEN ELIZABETH I, quoted by Francis Bacon in *Apophthegms*, 1625

Anger as well as love casts out fear.
> ━ MARGARET DELAND, *Small Things*, 1919

Anger makes us all stupid.
　—JOHANNA SPYRI, *Heidi*, 1881

I have a right to my anger, I don't want anybody telling me I shouldn't be, that it's not nice to be, and that something's wrong with me because I get angry.
　—MAXINE WATERS, in Brian Lanker's *I Dream a World*, 1989

Through anger, the truth looks simple.
　—JANE McCABE, in Carolyn Heilbrun's *Writing a Woman's Life*, 1988

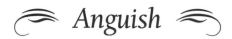 Anguish

The beauty of the world has two edges, one of laughter, one of anguish, cutting the heart asunder.
　—VIRGINIA WOOLF, *A Room of One's Own*, 1929

 Animals

Animals are such agreeable friends—they ask no questions, they pass no criticisms.
　—GEORGE ELIOT, *Scenes of Clerical Life*, 1880

Animals . . . do not suffer less because they have no words.
　—ANNA SEWELL, *Black Beauty*, 1877

Animals do not betray, they do not exploit, they do not oppress, they do not enslave, they do not sin. They have their being, and there being is honest, and who can say that of man?
　—TAYLOR CALDWELL, *Great Lions of God*, 1970

 *Anniversaries*

The punctuation of anniversaries is terrible, like the closing of doors, one after another between you and what you want to hold on to.
— ANNE MORROW LINDBERGH, diary entry on the first anniversary of her son's kidnapping and death, *Locked Rooms and Open Doors,* 1974

(*See also* Grief, Misery, Pain)

 *Anxiety*

Love looks forward, hate looks back, anxiety has eyes all over its head.
— MIGNON MCLAUGHLIN, *The Neurotic's Notebook,* 1963

Anxiety is love's greatest killer, because it is like the stranglehold of the drowning.
— ANAÏS NIN, *The Diary of Anaïs Nin,* 1974

Normal worrying is a natural safeguard, and we need it. The tigers out there are real, just as plentiful as ever, and better armed than they used to be.
— BARBARA HOLLAND, *One's Company,* 1992

(*See also* Worry)

Apathy

Science may have found a cure for most evils, but it has found no remedy for the worst of them all—the apathy of human beings.
— HELEN KELLER *My Religion*, 1974

Appearance

Why not be oneself? That is the whole secret of a successful appearance. If one is a greyhound why try to look like a Pekinese?
— EDITH SITWELL, *Why I Look As I Do*

The more legal and material hindrances women have broken through, the more strictly and heavily and cruelly images of female beauty have come to weigh upon them.
— NAOMI WOLF, *The Beauty Myth*, 1990

Nature gives you the face you have when you are twenty. Life shapes the face you have at thirty. But it is up to you to earn the face you have at fifty.
— COCO CHANEL, *Coco Chanel: Her Life, Her Secrets*, 1972

A woman can look both moral and exciting—if she also looks as if it was quite a struggle.
— EDNA FERBER, *Reader's Digest*, December 1954

Most plain girls are virtuous because of the scarcity of opportunity to be otherwise.
— MAYA ANGELOU, *I Know Why the Caged Bird Sings*, 1970

When the heart is in love, beauty is of no account.
— AFGHANISTAN PROVERB

I think I'm a bit better-looking than she is.

— PRINCESS ANNE, **after being told that she looked like Princess Anne, in Clifton Fadiman (ed)** *The Little, Brown Book of Anecdotes,* **1985**

Is it too much to ask that women be spared the daily struggle for superhuman beauty in order to offer it to the caresses of a subhumanly ugly mate?

— GERMAINE GREER, *The Female Eunuch,* 1970

There are no ugly women; only lazy ones.

— HELENA RUBENSTEIN, *My Life for Beauty,* 1966

Only the really plain people know about love—the very fascinating ones try so hard to create an impression that they soon exhaust their talents.

— KATHARINE HEPBURN, *Look,* February 18, 1958

I'm the female equivalent of a counterfeit $20 bill. Half of what you see is a pretty good reproduction, the rest is a fraud.

— CHER, *Star Speak: Hollywood on Everything,* 1987

(*See also* Beauty)

Applause

If nothing else, there's applause . . . like waves of love pouring over the footlights.

— EVE HARRINGTON in *All About Eve,* script by Joseph L. Mankiewicz, 1950

 *Art*

A work of art has an author, and yet when it is perfect, it has something which is anonymous about it.

— SIMONE WEIL, *Gravity and Grace,* 1952

Art is the only way to run away without leaving home.

— TWYLA THARP, *Push Comes to Shove,* 1992

Art does the same thing dreams do.

— JOYCE CAROL OATES, in *Newsweek,* 1970

Art in America has always been regarded as a luxury.

— HALLIE FLANAGAN, *Arena,* 1940

Art . . . does not take kindly to facts, is helpless to grapple with theories, and is killed outright by a sermon.

— AGNES REPPLIER, *Points of View,* 1891

It terrified me to have an idea that was solely mine to be no longer a part of my mind, but totally public.

— MAYA LIN, **on her design for Vietnam Veterans Memorial in Washington, DC,** *National Geographic,* **May 1985**

(*See also* Artist, Creativity)

 *Artists*

The work of art which I do not make, none other will ever make it.

— SIMONE WEIL, *The Notebooks of Simone Weil,* 1951

If I didn't start painting, I would have raised chickens.

— GRANDMA MOSES, *My Life's History,* **edited by Aotto Kallir, 1952**

Every artist is an unhappy lover.
 ━ IRIS MURDOCH, *The Black Prince,* 1973

The key is what is within the artist. The artist can only paint what she or he is about.
 ━ LEE KRASNER, in Eleanor Munro, *Originals: American Women Artists,* 1979

No artist is pleased. . . . There is only a queer divine dissatisfaction, a blessed unrest that keeps us marching and makes us more alive than the others.
 ━ MARTHA GRAHAM, in Agnes de Mille, *Dance to the Piper,* 1952

One has to have a bit of neurosis to go on being an artist. A balanced human seldom produces art. It's that imbalance which impels us.
 ━ BEVERLY PEPPER, in Eleanor Munro, *Originals: American Women Artists,* 1979

What an artist is for is to tell us what we see but do not know that we see.
 ━ EDITH SITWELL, in *Edith Sitwell,* 1976

No artist is ahead of this time. He *is* his time; it is just that others are behind the times.
 ━ MARTHA GRAHAM, in John Heilpern, "The Amazing Martha," *The Observer Magazine,* 1979

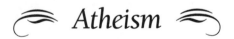 *Atheism*

No one is so thoroughly superstitious as the godless man.
 ━ HARRIET BEECHER STOWE, *Uncle Tom's Cabin,* 1852

# Aunts

The good aunt always gives to any kind of nieces and nephews the something extra, the something unexpected, the something which comes from outside the limits of their habitual world. She is an aviator from another country who drops leaflets out of the sky. She does not intend to start a revolution, she only wants them to learn that there are other countries besides their own.

— KATHARINE BUTLER HATHAWAY, *The Little Locksmith,* 1942

# Autocrats

I shall be an autocrat, that's my trade; and the good Lord will forgive me, that's his.

— CATHERINE THE GREAT, attributed

# Babies

They lie flat on their noses at first in what appears to be a drunken slumber, then flat on their backs kicking and screaming, demanding impossibilities in a foreign language.

— KATHERINE ANNE PORTER, "Marriage Is Belonging," *The Days Before* (1952)

The hot, moist smell of babies fresh from naps.

— BARBARA LAZEAR ASCHER, *Playing After Dark,* 1980

Lord knows what incommunicable small terrors infants go through, unknown to all.

— MARGARET DRABBLE, *The Millstone,* 1965

Like a round loaf . . .
I kneaded you, patted you,
greased you smooth, floured you.
— JUDITH TOTH, "The Newborn," in *Women Poets of the World,* 1983

For years we have given scientific attention to the care and rearing of plants and animals, but we have allowed babies to be raised chiefly by tradition.
— EDITH BELLE LOWRY, *False Modesty,* 1912

If you want a baby, have a new one. Don't baby the old one.
— JESSAMYN WEST, *To See the Dream,* 1957

Bachelors

In Mexico, a bachelor is a man who can't play the guitar.
— LILLIAN DAY, *Kiss and Tell,* 1931

Never trust a husband too far or a bachelor too near.
— HELEN ROWLAND, *The Rubaiyat of a Bachelor,* 1915

Summer bachelors, like summer breezes, are never as cool as they pretend to be.
— NORA EPHRON, *New York Post,* August 22, 1965

A bachelor is a man who can take a nap on top of a bedspread.
— MARCELENE COX, in *Ladies' Home Journal,* 1949

Somehow a bachelor never quite gets over the idea that he is a thing of beauty and a boy forever.
— HELEN ROWLAND, *A Guide to Men,* 1922

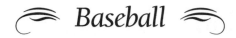

Baseball

For every man with a baseball story—a memory of a moment at the plate or in the field—there is a woman with a couldn't-play-baseball story.
— MARIAH BURTON NELSON, *Are We Winning Yet?* 1992

Pitching was about fooling people, manipulating them, making them believe in something that ultimately wasn't there. Great pitching was great lying.
— LINDA ELLERBEE, *Move on,* 1991

Baseball is . . . the world's most tranquil sport. It is probably the only active sport where you are not seriously required to be alive to play.
— NIKKI GIOVANNI, *Sacred Cows . . . and Other Edibles,* 1988

Beauty

Beauty more than bitterness makes the heart break.
— SARA TEASDALE, "Vignettes Overseas: Capri"

Beauty without the beloved is an arrow through the heart.
— UNKNOWN

What woman whose beauty time has at last ravaged can hear without tears the song that her lover once sung for her?
— MADAME DE STAËL, *Lettres sur les ouvrages et le caractere de J. J. Rousseau,* 1788

The most deeply moving element in the contemplation of beauty is the element of loss. We desire to hold; but the sunset melts into the night, and the secret of the painting on the wall can never be the secret of the buyer.

— PAMELA HANSFORD JOHNSON, *Catherine Carter,* 1958

If beauty is truth, why don't women go to the library to get their hair done?

— LILY TOMLIN, in Sally Feldman (ed) *Woman's Hour Book of Humour,* 1993

I'm tired of all this nonsense about beauty being only skin-deep. That's deep enough. What do you want—an adorable pancreas?

— JEAN KERR, *The Snake Has All the Lines,* 1958

The beauty myth moves for men as a mirage; its power lies in its ever-receding nature. When the gap is closed, the lover embraces only his own disillusion.

— NAOMI WOLF, *The Beauty Myth,* 1990

(*See also* Appearance)

Bed

Was it for this I uttered prayers
and sobbed and cursed and kicked the stairs,
That now, domestic as a plate,
I should retire at half-past eight?

— EDNA ST. VINCENT MILLAY, *Grown-Up,* 1920

The average, healthy well-adjusted adult gets up at 7:30 in the morning feeling just plain terrible.

— JEAN KERR, *Please Don't Eat the Daisies,* 1957

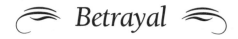

Betrayal

I saw this thing turn, like a flower, once picked, turning petals into bright knives in your hand. And it was so much desired, so lovely, that your fingers will not loosen, and you have only disbelief that this, of all you have ever known, should have the possibility of pain.
— NADINE GORDIMER, *The Lying Days*, 1953

If only one could tell true love from false love as one can tell mushrooms from toadstools.
— KATHERINE MANSFIELD, *Journal of Katherine Mansfield*, 1930

When one loves a certain way, even betrayals become unimportant.
— COLETTE, *Claudine and Annie*, 1903

(*See also* Anguish, Breaking Up, Infidelity)

Biology

Cells let us walk, talk, think, make love and realize the bath water is cold.
— LORRAINE LEE CUDMORE, *The Center of Life*, 1977

Birds

The silence and the solitude were touched by wild music, thin as air, the faraway gabbling of geese flying at night. Presently I caught sight of them as they streamed across the face of the moon . . . and suddenly I saw, in one of those rare moments of insight, what it means to be wild and free.
— MARTHA REBEN, *A Sharing of Joy*, 1963

I hope you love birds too. It's economical. It saves going to heaven.
— EMILY DICKINSON, *Letters of Emily Dickinson,* 1885

No sadder sound salutes you than the clear,
Wild laughter of the loon.
— CELIA THAXTER, "Seaward," *Poems,* 1872

A certain red cardinal sounded like a little bottle being filled up,
up, up with some clear liquid.
— ELIZABETH ENRIGHT, *Gone-Away Lake,* 1957

The wild geese were passing over. . . . There was an infinite cold
passion in their flight, like the passion of the universe, a proud
mystery never to be solved.
— MARTHA OSTENSO, *Wild Geese,* 1925

Birth Control

We want better reasons for having children than not knowing how
to prevent them.
— DORA RUSSELL, *Hypatia: or Women and Knowledge,* 1925

If women cannot plan their pregnancies, they can plan little else in
their lives.
— ALICE S. ROSSI, *The Feminist Papers,* 1973

Women have child-bearing equipment. To choose not to use the
equipment is no more blocking what is instinctive than it is for a
man who, muscles or no, chooses not to be a weight-lifter.
— BETTY ROLLIN, "Motherhood: Who Needs It?" in *Look,* 1970

A modern and human civilization must control conception or sink
into barbaric cruelty to individuals.
— MARIE STOPES, *Contraception,* 1923

No woman can call herself free who does not own and control her body. No woman can call herself free until she can choose consciously whether she will or will not be a mother.

— MARGARET H. SANGER, *Women and the New Race,* 1920

The greatest of all contraceptives is affluence.

— INDIRA GANDHI, *Freedom Is the Starting Point,* 1976

Through its prohibition on birth control, the Church has suggested that the only right way to have children is . . . a kind of forced labor culminating in the production of another soul for God. What kind of God stands like Lee Iacocca at the end of an assembly line, driving his workers with a greedy "More! More!" while the automobiles pile up in showrooms and on freeways and in used-car lots and finally junkyards, his only satisfaction the gross production figures at the end of every quarter?

— NANCY MAIRS, *Ordinary Time,* 1993

Bisexuality

Because our society is so polarized between homosexuals and heterosexuals, the bisexual closet has two doors.

— LORAINE HUTCHINS AND LANI KAAHUMANU, *Bi Any Other Name,* 1991

I came to live in a country I love; some people label me a defector. I have loved men and women in my life; I've been labeled "the bisexual defector." Want to know another secret? I'm even ambidextrous. I don't like labels. Just call me Martina.

— MARTINA NAVRATILOVA, *Martina Navratilova—Being Myself,* 1985

What is new is not bisexuality, but rather the widening of our awareness and acceptance of human capacities for sexual love.

— MARGARET MEAD in *Redbook,* 1975

(*See also* Homosexuality, Lesbians)

 Blacks

If growing up is painful for the Southern Black girl, being aware of her displacement is the rust on the razor that threatens the throat.
— MAYA ANGELOU, *I know Why the Caged Bird Sings*, 1969

The way I was taught, being black was a plus, always. Being a human being, being in America, and being black, all three were the greatest things that could happen to you. The combination was unbeatable.
— LEONTYNE PRICE, in *I Dream a World*, 1989

I tell you, Joe, little Willie said
Black is as tired as it is beautiful
— CAROLYN RODGERS, *how i got ovah*, 1975

It is utterly exhausting being Black in America—physically, mentally and emotionally. While many minority groups and women feel similar stress, there is no respite or escape from your badge of color.
— MARIAN WRIGHT EDELMAN, *The Measure of Our Success*, 1992

Raising Black children—female and male—in the mouth of a racist, sexist, suicidal dragon is perilous and chancy. If they cannot love and resist at the same time, they will probably not survive.
— AUDRE LORDE, "Man Child," in *Conditions*, 1979

The drums of Africa still beat in my heart. They will not let me rest while there is a single Negro boy or girl without a chance to prove his worth.
— MARY MCLEOD BETHUNE, in *Who, the Magazine About People*, 1941

It is not healthy when a nation lives within a nation, as colored Americans are living inside America. A nation cannot live confident of its tomorrow if its refugees are among its own citizens.
— PEARL S. BUCK, *What America Means to Me*, 1943

Black people are the only segment in American society that is defined by its weakest elements. Every other segment is defined by its highest achievement. We have to turn that around.
— JEWELL JACKSON McCABE, *I Dream a World*, 1989

Any woman who has a great deal to offer the world is in trouble. And if she's a black woman, she's in deep trouble.
— HAZEL SCOTT, in "Great (Hazel) Scott!" *Ms*, 1974

I speak to the black experience, but I am always talking about the human condition—about what we can endure, dream, fail at, and still survive.
— MAYA ANGELOU, quoted in *Current Biographies*, 1974

(*See also* Racism, Whites)

Blame

In the final analysis, each of us is responsible for what we are. We cannot blame it on our mothers, who, thanks to Freud, have replaced money as the root of all evil.
— HELEN LAWRENSON, *Stranger at the Party*, 1975

Blaming mother is just a negative way of clinging to her still.
— NANCY FRIDAY, *My Mother/My Self*, 1977

Books

There are books that one needs maturity to enjoy just as there are books an adult can come on too late to savor.
— PHYLLIS McGINLEY, *The Province of the Heart*, 1959

Books are like lobster shells; we surround ourselves with 'em, then we grow out of 'em and leave 'em behind, as evidence of our earlier stages of development.

— DOROTHY L. SAYERS, *The Unpleasantness at the Bellona Club,* 1928

Boredom

I'm afraid of nothing except being bored.

— GRETA GARBO to Robert Taylor in *Camille,* 1936

Breaking Up

Take me or leave me, or, as is the usual order of things, both.

— DOROTHY PARKER, "A Good Novel, and a Great Story," *The New Yorker,* 1928

(*See also* Betrayal, Divorce, Estrangement, Parting)

Canada

For some reason, a glaze passes over people's faces when you say "Canada."

— SONDRA GOTLEIB, wife of Canadian ambassador to the U.S., *New York Times,* July 8, 1982

If the national mental illness of the United States is megalomania, that of Canada is paranoid schizophrenia.

— MARGARET ATWOOD, *The Journals of Susanna Moodie,* 1970

Cats

Mr. Cat knows that a whisker spied is not a whole mouse.
— MARGUERITE HENRY, *San Domingo, the Medicine Hat Stallion*, 1972

Cats sleep fat and walk thin.
— ROSALIE MOORE, in *The New Yorker*, 1946

People are always commenting that you never know what cats are thinking. The observation tells us a little about cats and a lot more about people. It implies that people ought to know what other beings are thinking, and that cats violate this norm in some strange way. Why?
— ANNE MENDELSON, in Judy Fireman (ed) *Cat Catalog*, 1976

The more you talk to cats, the smarter they become. An occasional "nice kitty" will have no measurable effect; intelligent conversation is required.
— LILLIAN JACKSON BRAUN, *The Cat Who Knew Shakespeare*, 1988

Censorship

There is no danger in letting people have their say. . . . There is a danger when you try to stop them from saying it.
— HELEN GAHAGAN DOUGLAS, *A Full Life*, 1982

Perhaps those men in the House Caucus Room are determined to spread silence: to frighten those voices which will shout no, and ask questions, defend the few, attack cruelty and proclaim the rights and dignity of man. . . . America is going to look very strange to Americans and they will not be at home here, for the air will slowly become unbreathable to all forms of life except sheep.
— MARTHA GELLHORN, in *The New Republic*, 1947

I'm going to introduce a resolution to have the post master general stop reading dirty books and deliver the mail.

— SEN. GALE W. MCGEE, on efficiency over censorship, *Quote*,
September 13, 1959

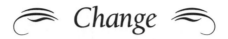 *Change*

So often I heard people paying blind obeisance to change—as though it had some virtue of its own. Change or we will die. Change or we will stagnate. Evergreens don't stagnate.

— JUDITH ROSSNER, *Nine Months in the Life of an Old Maid*, 1969

All birth is unwilling.

— PEARL S. BUCK, *What America Means to Me*, 1943

People change and forget to tell each other.

— LILLIAN HELLMAN, *Toys in the Attic*, 1960

People don't alter. They may with enormous difficulty modify themselves, but they never really change.

— MARGERY ALLINGHAM, *Safer than Love*, 1962

Old-fashioned ways which no longer apply to changed conditions are a snare in which the feet of women have always become readily entangled.

— JANE ADDAMS, "Utilization of Women in City Government" in
Newer Ideals of Peace, 1967

"Yes" I answered you last night;
"No" this morning, sir, I say:
Colors seen by candlelight
Will not look the same by day.

— ELIZABETH BARRETT BROWNING, *The Lady's "Yes,"* 1844

Charisma

Charisma without substance is a dangerous thing.
— KIM CAMPBELL, speech in British Columbia, October 22, 1986

Charity

What we are doing is just a drop in the ocean. But if that drop was not in the ocean, I think the ocean would be less because of that missing drop. I do not agree with the big way of doing things.
— MOTHER TERESA, *A Gift for God*, 1975

Women know the damnation of charity because the habit of civilization has always been to throw them cheap alms rather than give them good wages.
— DAME REBECCA WEST, *The Clarion*, December 13, 1912

To have and not to give is often worse than to steal.
— MARIE VON EBNER-ESCHENBACH, *Aphorisms*, 1893

The results of philanthropy are always beyond calculation.
— MIRIAM BEARD, *A History of Business*, 1938

You have no idea, sir, how difficult it is to be the victim of benevolence.
— JANE AIKEN HODGE, *Marry in Haste*, 1961

Pity and charity may be at root an attempt to propitiate the dark powers that have not touched us yet.
— MARILYNNE ROBINSON, *Housekeeping*, 1980

Charity has always been an expression of the guilty consciences of a ruling class.
— DORIS LESSING, *Children of Violence: A Proper Marriage*, 1954

 *Childbirth*

Having a baby is like suddenly getting the world's worst roommate, like having Janis Joplin with a bad hangover and PMS come to stay with you.
— ANNE LAMOTT, *Bird by Bird,* 1994

As often as I have witnessed the miracle, held the perfect creature with its tiny hands and feet, each time I have felt as though I were entering a cathedral with prayers in my heart.
— MARGARET SANGER, *Margaret Sanger,* 1958

If men had to have babies, they would only ever have one each.
— DIANA, PRINCESS OF WALES, in *The Observer,* 1984

The revolting details of childbirth had been hidden from me with such care that I was as surprised as I was horrified and I cannot help thinking that the vows most women are made to take are very foolhardy. I doubt whether they would willingly go to the altar to swear that they will allow themselves to be broken on the wheel every nine months.
— SUZANNE CURCHOD NECKER (1766), in J. Christopher Herold's *Mistress to an Age,* 1958

I think of birth as the search for a larger apartment.
— RITA MAE BROWN, *Starting from Scratch,* 1988

 *Childhood*

When it comes time to do your own life, you either perpetuate your childhood or you stand on it and finally kick it out from under.
— ROSELLEN BROWN, *Civil Wars,* 1984

I had the most satisfactory of childhoods because Mother, small, delicate-boned, witty, and articulate, turned out to be exactly my age.
— KAY BOYLE, in *Being Geniuses Together,* 1968

Remember your own childhood. That complete certainty you had, looking at the grownups, that you would never be like that. It was a lonely feeling, but euphoric, too.
— JANE CAMPION, *The Times Magazine,* January 1, 1994

But childhood prolonged cannot remain a fairyland. It becomes a hell.
— LOUISE BOGAN, on Katherine Mansfield, *Childhood's False Eden,* 1940

I believe that the experience of childhood is irretrievable. All that remains, for any of us, is a handful of brilliant frozen moments, already dangerously distorted by the wisdom of maturity.
— PENELOPE LIVELY, *Oleander, Jacaranda,* 1994

(*See also* Adolescence, Adulthood, Babies, Children, Daughters, Family, Fathers, Growing Up, Mothers, Mothers and Sons, Parenting, Teenagers, Youth)

Children

Children should be taught not the little virtues but the great ones. Not thrift but generosity and an indifference to money; not caution but courage and a contempt for danger; not a desire for success but a desire to be and to know.
— NATALIA GINZBURG, *The Little Virtues,* 1962

What feeling is so nice as a child's hand in yours? So small, so soft and warm, like a kitten huddling in the shelter of your clasp.
— MARJORIE HOLMES, *Calendar of Love and Inspiration,* 1981

Being constantly with children was like wearing a pair of shoes that were expensive and too small. She couldn't bear to throw them out, but they gave her blisters.

— BERYL BAINBRIDGE, *Injury Times,* 1977

Our children are not going to be just "our children"—they are going to be other people's husbands and wives and the parents of our grandchildren.

— MARY S. CALDERONE, NBC-TV, January 18, 1974

Thou, straggler into loving arms,
Young climber up of knees,
When I forget thy thousand ways,
Then life and all shall cease

— MARY LAMB, *Parental Recollections,* 1809

As soon as [children] develop a sense of humor and get to be good company, maybe even remember to take the trash out and close the refrigerator door, they pack up their electronic equipment and their clothes . . . and leave in a U-Haul.

— BARBARA HOLLAND, *One's Company,* 1992

(*See also* Adolescence, Babies, Childhood, Daughters, Fathers, Family, Growing Up, Mothers, Mothers-Daughters, Mothers and Sons, Parenting, Teenagers, Youth)

Christianity

Christianity is really a man's religion; there's not much in it for women except docility, obedience . . . downcast eyes and death in childbirth. For the men it's better: all power and money and fine robes, the burning of the heretics—fun, fun, fun!—and the Inquisition fulminating from the pulpit.

— FAY WELDON, *The Heart of the Country,* 1987

You don't have to be dowdy to be a Christian.
— TAMMY FAYE BAKKER, *Newsweek,* 1987

Christian ideology has contributed no little to the oppression of women.
— SIMONE DE BEAUVOIR, *The Second Sex,* 1949

Pagans deified life and Christians deified death.
— MADAME DE STAËL, *Corinne ou de l'Italie,* 1807

Authentic Christianity never destroys what is good. It makes it grow, transfigures it and enriches itself from it.
— CLAIRE HUCHET BISHOP, *France Alive,* 1947

Perhaps there was no greater crime as yet than all the lies Western civilization had told in the name of Jesus Christ.
— BESSIE HEAD, *When Rain Clouds Gather,* 1969

 *Christmas*

There is nothing sadder in this world than to wake Christmas morning and not be a child.
— ERMA BOMBECK, *I Lost Everything in the Postnatal Depression,* 1970

There are few sensations more painful than, in the midst of deep grief, to know that the season which we have always associated with mirth and rejoicing is at hand.
— MRS. SARAH J. HALE, *Traits of American Life,* 1835

No matter how many Christmas presents you give your child, there's always that terrible moment when he's opened the very last one. That's when he expects you to say, "Oh yes, I almost forgot," and take him out and show him the pony.
— MIGNON MCLAUGHLIN, *The Second Neurotic's Notebook,* 1966

Christmas is not an external event at all, but a piece of one's home that one carries in one's heart. Like a nursery story, its validity rests on exact repetition, so that it comes around every time as the evocation of one's whole life and particularly of the most distant bits of it in childhood.

— FREYA STARK, in *Time and Tide*, 1953

 *Church*

I make a distinction between the doctrines of the Church, which matter, and the structure invented by half a dozen Italians who got to be pope and which is of very little use to anybody.

— MARIE CORELLI, *The Master Christian*, 1900

It is a very rare church indeed that encourages its members to think for themselves in religious matters, or even tolerates this.

— ANNA ROE, *The Making of a Scientist*, 1952

If we go to church we are confronted with a system of begging so complicated and so resolute that all other demands sink into insignificance by its side.

— AGNES REPPLIER, in Emma Repplier, *Agnes Repplier*, 1957

She say, Celie, tell the truth, have you ever found God in church? I never did. I just found a bunch of folks hoping for him to show. Any God I ever felt in church I brought in with me.

— ALICE WALKER, *The Color Purple*, 1982

The Nurse knew why she disliked church services, for as she raised her head she observed that the Curate, and the Rector and the Archbishop were all men. The vergers were men; the organist was a man, the choir boys, the sidesmen and soloist and church wardens, all were men. The architects who had built the church, the composers of the music, the translators of the psalms, the compilers of the liturgy, all these too, the Nurse pondered, had been men.

— WINIFRED HOLTBY, *Truth Is Not Sober*, 1934

 *Class*

The upper classes are merely a nation's past; the middle class is its future.
— AYN RAND, in *The Ayn Rand Letter,* 1971

An aristocracy in a republic is like a chicken whose head has been cut off; it may run about in a lively way, but in fact it is dead.
— NANCY MITFORD, *Noblesse Oblige,* 1956

Being in the middle class is a feeling as well as an income level.
— MARGARET HALSEY, *The Folks at Home,* 1952

To fear the bourgeois is bourgeois.
— MAUREEN HOWARD, *Facts of Life,* 1978

 *Clothes*

Where's the man could ease a heart
Like a satin gown?
— DOROTHY PARKER, "The Satin Dress," *Literary Digest,* February 13, 1926

If you can't dress for success, at least dress for trying.
— LYNNE ALPERN AND ESTHER BLUMENFELD, *Oh, Lord, I Sound Just Like Mamma,* 1986

Hats divide generally into three classes: offensive hats, defensive hats, and shrapnel.
— KATHARINE WHITEHORN, *Shouts and Murmurs,* 1963

I base most of my fashion sense on what doesn't itch.
— GILDA RADNER, *It's Always Something,* 1989

There comes a time when you have to let your clothes go out in the world and try to make it on their own.
— BETTE MIDLER, *People*, August 31, 1970

Your clothes speak even before you do.
— JACQUELINE MURRAY, WITH TONI NEBEL, *The Power of Dress*, 1989

Clothes never shut up.
— SUSAN BROWNMILLER, *Femininity*, 1984

She knew someday she would find the exact right outfit that would make her life work. Maybe not her whole life, she thought as she got back in bed, but at least the parts she had to dress for.
— CARRIE FISHER, *Postcards from the Edge*, 1987

Any garment that makes you feel bad will make you look bad.
— VICTORIA BILLINGS, *The Womanbook*, 1974

She spotted an Adolofo suit in that shade of tan that comes from mixing taste with being born with a great deal of money.
— JUDITH KELMAN, *Hush Little Darlings*, 1989

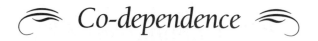

Co-dependence

Those who make some other person their job are dangerous.
— DOROTHY L. SAYERS, *Gaudy Night*, 1935

There are only two states of being in the world of codependency— recovery and denial.
— WENDY KAMINER, *I'm Dysfunctional, You're Dysfunctional*, 1992

People who are always thinking of the feelings of others can be very destructive because they are hiding so much from themselves.
— MAY SARTON, *Crucial Conversations*, 1975

Codependence is taking someone else's temperature to see how you feel.
— LINDA ELLERBEE, *Move On*, 1991

Our love relationships have been based on the pathological model that two persons who pair will become one. Because this model does not allow for separateness in relationships, it has fostered dependency.
— MARILYN MASON, in *Co-Dependency*, 1984

 *Coffee*

Coffee: We can get it anywhere, and get as loaded as we like on it, until such teeth-chattering, eye-bulging, nonsense-gibbering time as we may be classified unable to operate heavy machinery.
— JOAN FRANK, in *The San Francisco Examiner*, 1991

There was a tiny range within which coffee was effective, short of which it was useless, and beyond which, fatal.
— ANNIE DILLARD, *The Writing Life*, 1989

 *Committees*

Any committee is only as good as the most knowledgeable, determined and vigorous person on it. There must be somebody who provides the flame.
— LADY BIRD JOHNSON, *A White House Diary*, 1970

Competition

The trouble with the rat race is that even if you win, you're still a rat.
— LILY TOMLIN, **attributed**

I don't have to be enemies with someone to be competitors with them.
— JACKIE JOYNER-KERSEE **in Mariah Burton Nelson,** *Are We Winning Yet?*, 1991

Even in misery we love to be foremost, to have the bitter in our cup acknowledged as more bitter than that of others.
— MRS. OLIPHANT, *A House in Bloomsbury,* 1894

Computers

If one ox could not do the job they did not try to grow a bigger ox, but used two oxen. When we need greater computer power, the answer is not to get a bigger computer, but . . . to build systems of computers and operate them in parallel.
— GRACE MURRAY HOPPER, **speech,** 1987

Confidence

Success breeds confidence. But who has a right to confidence except the gods?
— BERYL MARKHAM, *West with the Night,* 1983

Confidence is a plant of slow growth.
— ANNA LEONOWENS, *The Romance of the Harem,* 1872

I am filled with confidence, not that I shall succeed in worldly things, but that even when things go badly for me, I shall still find life good and worth living.

— ETTY HILLESUM, *An Interrupted Life*, 1983

 *Conformity*

I think the reward for conformity is that everyone likes you except yourself.

— RITA MAE BROWN, *Bingo*, 1988

Only dead fish swim with the stream.

— LINDA ELLERBEE, *Move On*, 1991

 *Contentment*

And what do all the great words come to in the end, but that?—I love you—I am at rest with you—I have come home.

— DOROTHY L. SAYERS, *Busman's Honeymoon*, 1937

(*See also* Happiness, Joy)

 *Controversy*

There are two sides to every issue: one side is right and the other is wrong, but the middle is always evil.

— AYN RAND, *Atlas Shrugged*, 1957

Conversation

A gossip is one who talks to you about others; a bore is one who talks to you about himself; and a brilliant conversationalist is one who talks to you about yourself.

— LISA KIRK, *New York Journal-American*, March 9, 1954

Cooking

Non-cooks think it's silly to invest two hours' work in two minutes' enjoyment; but if cooking is evanescent, well, so is the ballet.

— JULIA CHILD, on NBC-TV, December 1, 1966

My mother was a good recreational cook, but what she basically believed about cooking was that if you worked hard and prospered, someone else would do it for you.

— NORA EPHRON, news summaries, December 31, 1983

Artur has his piano. I play my sonatas on the stove.

— NELLA RUBINSTEIN, in Elsa Maxwell, *How to Do It,* 1957

Cooking is like love. It should be entered into with abandon or not at all.

— HARRIET VAN HORNE, in *Vogue,* October 15, 1956

(*See also* Eating, Food, Wine)

Corporate Life

I never go out of my way to screw someone, but I'm always looking over my shoulder.

— KAREN VALENSTEIN, in "Against the Odds," *New York Times,* January 6, 1985

Today's corporate family is headed by a "father" who finds the child he never had, the child he always wanted, at the office and guides him (and sometimes her) up the ladder.

— PAULA BERNSTEIN, *Family Ties, Corporate Bonds,* 1985

The feminist surge will crest when a lady named Arabella, flounces and ruffles and all, can rise to the top of a Fortune 500 Corporation.

— ALMA DENNY, *New York Times,* August 30, 1985

Courage

The only courage that matters is the kind that gets you from one moment to the next.

— MIGNON MCLAUGHLIN, *The Second Neurotic's Notebook,* 1966

The success of life, the formation of character, is in proportion to the courage one has to say to one's own self: "Thou shalt not."

— CARRY NATION, *The Use and Need of the Life of Carry A. Nation,* 1905

I wanted you to see what real courage is, instead of getting the idea that courage is a man with a gun in his hand. It's when you know you're licked before you begin but you begin anyway and you see it through no matter what.

— HARPER LEE, *To Kill a Mockingbird,* 1966

There are all kinds of courage. It takes a great deal of bravery to stand up to our enemies—but just as much to stand up to our friends.
— J. K. ROWLING, *Harry Potter and the Sorcerer's Stone*, 1998

It takes far less courage to kill yourself than it takes to make yourself wake up one more time.
— JUDITH ROSSNER, *Nine Months in the Life of an Old Maid*, 1969

How cool, how quiet is true courage!
— FANNY BURNEY, *Evelina*, 1778

It is only in his head that man is heroic; in the pit of his stomach he is always a coward.
— MARY ROBERTS RINEHART, *The Red Lamp*, 1925

I think you always feel braver in another language.
— ANITA BROOKNER, in *The Observer*, August 7, 1988

The truly fearless think of themselves as normal.
— MARGARET ATWOOD, *Bluebeard's Egg*, 1986

Courage! I have shown it for years; think you I shall lose it at the moment when my sufferings are to end?
— MARIE ANTOINETTE, on the way to the guillotine, 1793

Courage is very important. Like a muscle, it is strengthened by use.
— RUTH GORDON, *L'Officiel*, Summer 1980

It's better to be a lion for a day than a sheep all your life.
— ELIZABETH KENNY, *Sister Kenny* by Victor Cohn, 1976

This is the art of courage: to see things as they are and still believe that the victory lies not with those who avoid the bad, but those who taste, in living awareness, every drop of the good.
— VICTORIA LINCOLN, "The Art of Courage," *Vogue*, October 1, 1952

Creativity

The creative impulse, like love, can be killed, but it cannot be taught.
— MADELEINE L'ENGLE, *A Circle of Quiet*, 1972

Creativity comes from trust. Trust your instincts. And never hope more than you work.
— RITA MAE BROWN, *Starting From Scratch*, 1988

Creative minds always have been known to survive any kind of bad training.
— ANNA FREUD, speech, 1968

I invented this rule for myself to be applied to every decision I might have to make in the future. I would sort out all the arguments and see which belonged to fear and which to creativeness, and other things being equal I would make the decision which had the larger number of creative reasons on its side. I think it must be a rule something like this that makes jonquils and crocuses come pushing through cold mud.
— KATHARINE BUTLER HATHAWAY, *The Little Locksmith*, 1942

Those who create are rare; those who cannot are numerous. Therefore, the latter are stronger.
— COCO CHANEL, in *This Week*, August 20, 1961

Culture

Knowledge of another culture should sharpen our ability to scrutinize more steadily, to appreciate more lovingly, our own.
— MARGARET MEAD, *Coming of Age in Samoa*, 1928

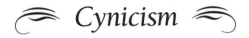 *Cynicism*

Cynicism is an unpleasant way of saying the truth.
— LILLIAN HELLMAN, *The Little Foxes*, 1939

Cynicism is the trademark of failure.
— KATHERINE CECIL THURSTON, *The Masquerader*, 1904

 *Dancing*

A good education is usually harmful to a dancer. A good calf is better than a good head.
— AGNES DE MILLE, news summaries, February 1, 1954

It occurred to me when I was 13 and wearing gloves and Mary Janes and going to dancing school, that no one should have to dance backward all their lives.
— JILL RUCKELSHAUS, *The Penguin Book of Women's Humour*, 1996

 *Dating*

A woman without a man cannot meet a man, any man, of any age, without thinking, even if it's for a half-second, perhaps this is the man.
— DORIS LESSING, *The Golden Notebook*, 1962

She'll throw herself at his head until he loses consciousness, and then she'll marry him.
— RUTH SAWYER, *The Primrose Ring*, 1915

I've got a heart like a college prom. Each one I dance with seems the best of all.
— ILKA CHASE, *In Bed We Cry,* 1943

When someone asks, "Why do you think he's not calling me?" there's always one answer—"He's not interested." There's not ever any other answer.
— FRAN LEBOWITZ, in *Mirabella,* 1992

I don't want anyone to notice that I've been chucked, well, not even chucked, to be chucked you have to have been going out with someone. I've been . . . sort of sampled.
— ARABELLA WEIR, *Does My Bum Look Big in This?* 1997

Everyone knows that dating in your thirties is not the happy-go-lucky free-for-all it was when you were twenty-two.
— HELEN FIELDING, *Bridget Jones' Diary,* 1996

There are very few of us who have heart enough to be really in love without encouragement. In nine cases out of ten, a woman had better show more affection than she feels.
— JANE AUSTEN, *Pride and Prejudice,* 1813

We've got to have
We plot to have
For it's so dreary not to have
That certain thing called the Boy Friend
— SANDY WILSON, *The Boyfriend,* 1954 song

It's amazing how much time and money can be saved in the world of dating by close attention to detail. A white sock here, a pair of red braces there, a grey slip-on shoe, a swastika, are as often as not all one needs to tell you there's no point in writing down phone numbers and forking out for expensive lunches because it's never going to be a runner.
— HELEN FIELDING, *Bridget Jones's Diary,* 1996

(*See also* Affairs, First Love, Free Love, Love, Loving, Love vs. Hate, Love vs. Like, Love Letters, Mature Love, May-December Romance, Memories of Love, True Love, Unrequited Love)

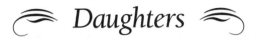

Daughters

Our attractiveness dries as theirs blooms, our journey shortens just as theirs begins. We too must be afraid and awed and amazed that we cannot live forever and that our replacements are eager for their turn, indifferent to our wishes, ready to leave us behind.
— ANNE ROIPHE, *Lovingkindness,* 1987

Being a daughter is only half the equation; bearing one is the other.
— ERICA JONG, *Parachutes & Kisses,* 1984

Death

You don't get to choose how you're going to die. Or when. You can only decide how you're going to live. Now.
— JOAN BAEZ, *Daybreak,* 1966

Watching a peaceful death of a human being reminds us of a falling star; one of a million lights in a vast sky that flares up for a brief moment only to disappear into the endless night forever.
— ELISABETH KÜBLER-ROSS, *On Death and Dying,* 1969

To the well-organized mind, death is but the next great adventure.
— J. K. ROWLING, in *Harry Potter and the Sorcerer's Stone,* 1998

Like a bird out of our hand,
Like a light out of our heart
You are gone
— H. D., "*Hymen,*" *Collected Poems,* 1925

". . . as they die, the ones we love, we lose our witnesses, our watchers, those who know and understand the tiny little meaningless patterns, those words drawn in water with a stick. And there is nothing left but the endless flow."

— ANNE RICE, *The Witching Hour,* 1990

Gracious dying is a huge, macabre and expensive joke on the American public.

— JESSICA MITFORD, on funeral directors, *The American Way of Death,* 1963

Death . . . is not more than passing from one room into another. But there's a difference for me, you know. Because in that other room, I shall be able to see.

— HELEN KELLER, recalled on her death, June 1, 1968

Death is terrifying because it is so ordinary.

— SUSAN CHEEVER, on her father's last illness, *Home Before Dark,* 1984

When I am dead and over me bright April
Shakes out her rain-drenched hair,
Though you should lean above me
Broken-hearted,
I shall not care.

— SARA TEASDALE, "I Shall Not Care," *Rivers to the Sea,* 1915

I postpone death by living, by suffering, by error, by risking, by giving, by losing.

— ANAÏS NIN, *Diary,* March 1933

Dying
Is an art, like everything else.
I do it exceptionally well.

— SYLVIA PLATH, *Lady Lazarus,* 1966

You learn something the day you die. You learn how to die.

— KATHERINE ANNE PORTER, recalled on her death, September 18, 1980

Dig my grave for two, with a stone to show it,
And on the stone write my name:
If he never comes, I shall never know it,
But sleep on all the same.

— CHRISTINA ROSSETTI, *Hoping Against Hope*

Every arrival foretells a leave-taking; every birth a death. Yet each death and departure comes to us as a surprise, a sorrow never anticipated.

— JESSAMYN WEST, *The Life I Really Lived,* 1979

People living deeply have no fear of death.

— ANAÏS NIN, *Diary,* 1967

I love thee with a love I seemed to lose
With my lost saints—I love thee with the breath,
Smiles, tears, of all my life!—and, if God choose,
I shall but love thee better after death.

— ELIZABETH BARRETT BROWNING, *Sonnets from the Portuguese,* 1850

(*See also* Grief; Immortality; Mother, Death of; Parting; Suicide)

Delicacy

Delicacy is to love what grace is to beauty.

— FRANÇOISE D'AUBIGNÉ DE MAINTENON, in *Uncommon Scold,* by Abby Adams, 1989

Depression

Once it wraps us in its damp gray arms, depression is hard to shake. Better to keep our lives stirred up . . . rather like a farm wife flapping her apron and waving her arms to keep the crows from settling onto the cornfield.
— BARBARA HOLLAND, *One's Company*, 1992

Desire

How helpless we are, like netted birds, when we are caught by desire!
— BELVA PLAIN, *Evergreen*, 1978

It is human nature to overestimate the thing you've never had.
— ELLEN GLASGOW, *The Romantic Comedians*, 1926

She went on gazing at Leonidas with the expression of a six year old contemplating a large slice of chocolate cake.
— SARAH CAUDWELL, *The Shortest Way to Hades*, 1984

The absolute yearning of one human body for another particular one and its indifference to substitutes is one of life's major mysteries.
— IRIS MURDOCH, *The Black Prince*, 1973

You can have anything you want if you want it desperately enough. You must want it with an inner exuberance that erupts through the skin and joins the energy that created the world.
— SHEILAH GRAHAM, *The Rest of the Story*, 1964

 *Dessert*

Cheese for dessert is rather like *Paradise Lost* in that everyone thinks he ought to like it, but still you don't notice too many people actually curling up with it.

— PEG BRACKEN, *The I Hate to Cook Book*, 1960

 *Diet*

On this twelfth day of my diet, I would rather die satiated than slim.

— MARGE PIERCY, *Stone, Paper, Knife*, 1983

 *Dieting*

Give me a dozen heartbreaks if you think it would help me lose one pound.

— COLETTE, *Chéri*, 1920

 *Differences*

To be alone is to be different; to be different is to be alone.

— SUZANNE GORDON, *Lonely in America*, 1976

Divorce

Divorce is the psychological equivalent of a triple coronary bypass. After such a monumental assault on the heart, it takes years to amend all the habits and attitudes that led up to it.

— MARY KAY BLAKELY, quoted in *Parade,* July 12, 1987

I doubt if there is one married person on earth who can be objective about divorce. It is always a threat, admittedly or not, and such a dire threat that it is almost a dirty word.

— NORA JOHNSON, *Atlantic,* July 1962

Divorce is like an amputation. You survive, but there is less of you.

— MARGARET ATWOOD, in *Time,* 1973

A lawyer is never entirely comfortable with a friendly divorce, any more than a good mortician wants to finish his job and then have the patient sit up on the table.

— JEAN KERR, *Time,* April 14, 1961

So many people think divorce a panacea for every ill, who find out, when they try it, the remedy is worse than the disease.

— DOROTHY DIX, *Dorothy Dix, Her Book,* 1926

Divorce is only less painful than the need for divorce.

— JANE O'REILLY, *The Girl I Left Behind,* 1980

Being divorced is like being hit by a Mack truck. If you live through it, you start looking very carefully to the right and to the left.

— JEAN KERR, *Mary, Mary,* 1963

(*See also* Betrayal, Divorce, Estrangement, Parting)

Dogs

I sometimes look into the face of my dog Stan and see wistful sadness and existential angst, when all he is actually doing is slowly scanning the ceiling for flies.

— MERRILL MARKOE, *What the Dogs Have Taught Me*, 1992

Bonny isn't ordinary. She has a liquid, intellectual gaze, as if she's not a dog but a Democrat, interested, like Gabe and Len, in civil liberties.

— LAURA CUNNINGHAM, *Sleeping Arrangements*, 1989

Dogs act exactly the way we would act if we had no shame.

— CYNTHIA HEIMEL, *Get Your Tongue Out of My Mouth, I'm Kissing You Goodbye*, 1993

Arnold was a dog's dog. Whenever he shuffled along walks and through alleyways, he always gave the impression of being onto something big.

— MARTHA GRIMES, *The Old Fox Deceiv'd*, 1982

If there is no God for thee
Then there is no God for me

— ANNA HEMPSTEAD BRANCH, "To a Dog," *Sonnets From a Lock Box*, 1929

Dogs believe they are human. Cats believe they are God.

— COLETTE, *Recollections*, 1986

 *Dreams*

I've dreamt in my life dreams that have stayed with me ever after, and changed my ideas: they've gone through and through me, like wine through water, and altered the colour of my mind.
— EMILY BRONTË, *Wuthering Heights*, 1847

Dreams are necessary to life.
— ANAÏS NIN, *The Diary of Anaïs Nin*, 1967

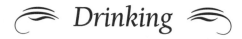 *Drinking*

One reason I don't drink is that I want to know when I am having a good time.
— NANCY ASTOR, in *Reader's Digest*, 1960

Nobody ever stops drinking until the cost of drinking becomes higher than the cost of not-drinking.
— ISABELLE HOLLAND, *The Long Search*, 1990

You can't drown your troubles, because troubles can swim.
— MARGARET MILLER, *Ask for Me Tomorrow*, 1976

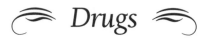 *Drugs*

Cocaine isn't habit-forming; I should know. I've been using it for years.
— LILLIAN HELLMAN, *Pentimento*, 1962

 Eating

How to eat spinach like a child: Divide into piles. Rearrange again into piles. After five or six maneuvers, sit back and say you're full.

— DELIA EPHRON, *New York Times,* 1983

Cantonese will eat anything in the sky but airplanes, anything in the sea but submarines and anything with four legs but the table.

— AMANDA BENNETT, *Wall Street Journal,* October 4, 1983

Depending on our age or social status, we eat things simply because they're there, like hamburgers, or because the lower classes haven't heard of them yet or wouldn't touch them with a barge pole, like radicchio and sushi.

— BARBARA HOLLAND, *One's Company,* 1922

You are eating the sea, that's it, only the sensation of a gulp of sea-water has been wafted out of it by some sorcery, and are on the verge of remembering you don't know what, mermaids or the sudden smell of kelp on the ebb tide or a poem you read once, something connected with the flavor of life itself.

— ELEANOR CLARK, *The Oysters of Locmariaquer,* 1964

We can only love a person who eats what we eat.

— RIGOBERTA MENCHU, in Elisabeth Burgos-Debray (ed), *I, Rigoberta Menchu,* 1983

One cannot think well, love well, sleep well, if one has not dined well.

— VIRGINIA WOOLF, *A Room of One's Own,* 1929

(*See also* Cooking, Dessert, Food, Wine)

Education

Those who have been required to memorize the world as it is will never create the world as it might be.

— JUDITH GROCH, *The Right to Create*, 1969

Intellectual freedom implies intellectual diversity.

— FRANCES FITZGERALD, *Fire in the Lake*, 1972

I saw in my own education some of the things which eat the power out of women.

— DAME REBECCA WEST, in *The Clarion*, February 14, 1913

The first rule of education is that if somebody will fund it, somebody will do it. The second rule of education is that once something is funded, workbooks will follow.

— SUSAN OHANIAN, *Ask Ms. Class*, 1996

All schoolchildren are hostages to red tape and fiscal insufficiency.

— ROSELLEN BROWN, *Civil Wars*, 1984

We must not, in trying to think about how we can make a big difference, ignore the small daily differences we can make which, over time, add up to big differences that we often cannot foresee.

— MARIAN WRIGHT EDELMAN, *Families in Peril*, 1987

I'm never going to be a movie star. But then, in all probability, Liz Taylor is never going to teach first and second grade.

— MARY J. WILSON, *Newsweek*, July 4, 1976

To be able to be caught up into the world of thought—that is educated.

— EDITH HAMILTON, *Saturday Evening Post*, September 27, 1958

(*See also* Intelligence)

Ego

It is far more impressive when others discover your good qualities without your help.

— JUDITH MARTIN, in *Readers' Digest*

Elegance

Elegance is not the prerogative of those who have just escaped from adolescence, but of those who have already taken possession of their future.

— COCO CHANEL, *McCalls*, November 1965

(*See also* Fashion)

Emotions

No emotion is the final one.

— JEANETTE WINTERSON, *Oranges Are Not the Only Fruit*, 1985

A belief which does not spring from a conviction of the emotions is no belief at all.

— EVELYN SCOTT, *Escapade*, 1923

Spilling your guts is just exactly as charming as it sounds.

— FRAN LEBOWITZ, *Social Studies*, 1977

Those who don't know how to weep with their whole heart don't know how to laugh, either.

— GOLDA MEIR, *Ms*, 1973

If you haven't had at least a slight poetic crack in the heart, you have been cheated by nature.

➤ PHYLLIS BATTELLE, in *New York Journal-American*, June 1, 1962

To have felt too much is to end in feeling nothing.

➤ DOROTHY THOMPSON, **on waiting in the courthouse for divorce from Sinclair Lewis, in Vincent Sheen,** *Dorothy and Red,* 1963

You have too many feelings, but not nearly enough love.

➤ EVELYN UNDERHILL (1909), IN CHARLES WILLIAMS (ED) *THE LETTERS OF EVELYN UNDERHILL,* 1943

(*See also* Affairs, Dating, First Love, Free Love, Love, Love Versus Hate, Love Versus Like, Love Letters, Loving, Mature Love, May-December Romance, Memories of Love, True Love, Unrequited Love)

End of Love

After all, my erstwhile dear
My no longer cherished
Need we say it was not there
Just because it perished?

➤ EDNA ST. VINCENT MILLAY, **"Passer Mortuus Est,"** *Second April,* 1921

When love turns away, now, I don't follow it. I sit and suffer, unprotesting, until I feel the tread of another step.

➤ SYLVIA ASHTON-WARNER, *Teacher,* 1963

How do you know that love is gone? If you said you would be there at seven, you get there by nine and he or she has not called the police yet—it's gone.

➤ MARLENE DIETRICH, *Marlene Dietrich's ABC,* 1962

Love never dies quite suddenly. He complains a great deal before expiring.

— MINNA THOMAS ANTRIM, *Sweethearts and Beaux,* 1905

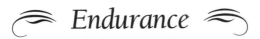

Endurance

As only New Yorkers know, if you can get through the twilight, you'll live through the night.

— DOROTHY PARKER, *Esquire,* November 1964

Enemies

Scratch a lover and find a foe.

— DOROTHY PARKER, *Enough Rope,* 1926

Prudence advises us to use our enemies as if one day they would be friends.

— MARGUERITE DE VALOIS, *Memoirs,* 1928

Lifelong enemies are, I think, as hard to make and as important to one's well-being as friends.

— JESSICA MITFORD, *The Making of a Muckraker,* 1979

Entertaining

With my little dinners I like to feel I am helping to save Western civilization.

— GWEN CAFRITZ, on her Washington dinner parties, *Quote,* January 8, 1967

Entertaining is one way of avoiding people.

— ELIZABETH BIBESCO, *The Fir and the Palm,* 1924

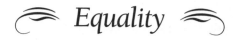

Equality

Fetters of gold are still fetters, and the softest lining can never make them so easy as liberty.

— MARY ASTELL, *An Essay in Defence of the Fairer Sex,* 1696

Until a woman is free to be as incompetent as the average male, then she will never be completely equal.

— ROSEANNA CUNNINGHAM, **by-election campaign speech,** May 1995

I ask no favors for my sex. All I ask of our brethren is that they will take their feet from off our necks.

— SARAH M. GRIMKÉ, *Letters on the Equality of the Sexes and the Condition of Women,* 1838

There will never be complete equality until women themselves help to make laws and to elect lawmakers.

— SUSAN B. ANTHONY, in *The Arena*

Whatever class and race divergences exist, top cats are tom cats.

— ELIZABETH JANEWAY, *Improper Behavior,* 1987

If absolute sovereignty be not necessary in a State, how comes it to be so in a family?

— MARY ASTELL, *Some Reflections upon Marriage,* 1706

If all men are born free, how is it that all women are born slaves?

— ASTELL, *ibid.*

Establishment

The establishment is made up of little men, very frightened.

— BELLA ABZUG, in *Bella!* by Mel Ziegler, 1972

Estrangement

There was no passion in her feeling for him, and no relief from its daily pressure. It was like being loved by a large, moist sponge.
— PHYLLIS BOTTOME, "The Other Island," *Strange Fruit,* 1928

(*See also* Betrayal, Breaking Up, Divorce, Parting)

Excellence

The secret of joy in work is contained in one word—excellence. To know how to do something well is to enjoy it.
— PEARL S. BUCK, *THE JOY OF CHILDREN,* 1964

When we do the best that we can, we never know what miracle is wrought in our life, or in the life of another.
— HELEN KELLER, *Out of the Dark,* 1914

Existence

An atom tossed in a chaos made
Of yeasting worlds, which bubble and foam.
Whence have I come?
What would be my home?
I hear no answer. I am afraid!
— AMY LOWELL, *Sword Blades and Poppy Seeds,* 1914

 *Experience*

Why do we spend years using up our bodies to nurture our minds with experience and find our minds turning then to our exhausted bodies for solace?

— ZELDA FITZGERALD and ALABAMA BEGGS, in *Save Me the Waltz,* 1932

Experience is a good teacher, but she sends in terrific bills.

— MINNA THOMAS ANTRIM, *Naked Truth and Veiled Illusions,* 1902

Experience is what really happens to you in the long run; the truth that finally overtakes you.

— KATHERINE ANNE PORTER, *The Collected Essays and Occasional Writings of Katherine Anne Porter,* 1970

Experience is a comb life gives you after you lose your hair.

— JUDITH STERN, in Bennett Cerf, *The Laugh's on Me,* 1959

Experience is never at bargain price.

— ALICE B. TOKLAS, *The Alice B. Toklas Cookbook,* 1954

 *Failure*

Failure is terribly important . . . the notion that failure is a negative thing is wrong.

— EMMA THOMPSON, *Vanity Fair,* February 1996

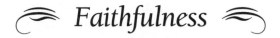 *Faithfulness*

Entreat me not to leave thee, or to return from following after thee; for whither thou goest, I will go; and where thou lodgest, I will lodge; thy people shall be my people, and thy God, my God. Where thou diest, will I die, and there will I be buried: the Lord do so to me, and more also, if aught but death part thee and me.

— THE BOOK OF RUTH 1:16–17

There is always something left to love. And if you haven't learned that, you ain't learned nothing.

— LORRAINE HANSBERRY, *A Raisin in the Sun*, 1959

(*See also* Affairs, Dating, First Love, Free Love, Love, Love Letters, Loving, Mature Love, May-December Romance, Memories of Love, True Love, Unrequited Love)

 *Fame*

Fame is a pearl many dive for and only a few bring up. Even when they do, it is not perfect, and they sigh for more, and lose better things in struggling for them.

— LOUISA MAY ALCOTT, *Jo's Boys*, 1886

So this was fame at last! Nothing but a vast debt to be paid to the world in energy, blood and time.

— MAY SARTON, *Mrs. Stevens Hears the Mermaids Singing*, 1965

I'm never going to be famous. My name will never be writ large on the roster of Those Who Do Things. I don't do anything. Not one single thing. I used to bite my nails, but I don't even do that anymore.

— DOROTHY PARKER, *The Little Hours*, 1941

I have pursued fame always in the hope of winning her love.
— MADAME DE STAËL, *Corinne ou de l'Italie*, 1807

Mere wealth, I am above it
It is the reputation wide
The playwright's group, the poet's pride
That eagerly I covet.
— PHYLLIS McGINLEY, *A Ballad of Anthologies*, 1941

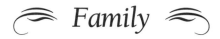 *Family*

The presidency is temporary, but the family is permanent.
— YVONNE DE GAULLE, **on her priorities as wife of French President Charles de Gaulle, quoted by Richard M. Nixon,** *RN: Memoirs of Richard Nixon*, 1978

Family traits, like murder, will out. Nature has but so many molds.
— LOUISE IMOGEN GUINEY, *Goose-Quill Papers*, 1885

You think you have a handle on God, the Universe, and the Great White Light until you go home for Thanksgiving. In an hour, you realize how far you've got to go and who is the real turkey.
— SHIRLEY MacLAINE, *Dance While You Can*, 1991

With relatives, long distance is even better than being there.
— LYNNE ALPERN and ESTHER BLUMENFELD, *Oh, Lord, I Sound Just Like Mamma*, 1986

To my way of thinking, the American family started to decline when parents began to communicate with their children. When we began to "rap," "feed into one another," "let things hang out," we heard things that mother didn't know about and would rather not.
— ERMA BOMBECK, *If Life Is a Bowl of Cherries—What Am I Doing in the Pits?* 1978

His biographers will tell how he helped the porter by drawing his own water, but no one will know that he never once thought to give his wife a moment's rest, or his sick child a drink of water. In 32 years, he never once sat for five minutes by his sick child's bedside.

— SONYA TOLSTOY, on her husband Leo, *Love and Hatred: The Stormy Marriage of Leo and Sonya Tolstoy,* 1994

(*See also* Adolescence, Babies, Childhood, Children, Daughters, Family, Fathers, Grandparents, Growing Up, Mothers, Mothers-Daughters, Mothers and Sons, Parenting, Siblings, Sisters, Teenagers, Youth)

Famous Women on Love

He spoke of love and the Supreme Court.

— ELIZABETH BLACK, on marriage proposal from Supreme Court Justice Hugo L. Black, *Christian Science Monitor,* February 27, 1986

Charles is life itself—pure life, force, like sunlight—and it is for this that I married him and this that holds me to him, caring always, caring desperately what happens to him and whatever he happens to be involved in.

— ANNE MORROW LINDBERGH, *War Within and Without,* 1980

P.S. It's all gossip about the prince. I'm not in the habit of taking my girlfriends' beaux.

— WALLIS (WARFIELD SIMPSON), Duchess of Windsor, letter to her aunt, February 18, 1934

Lyndon was the most outspoken, straightforward, determined person I'd ever encountered. I knew I'd met something remarkable—but I didn't know quite what.

— CLAUDIA "LADY BIRD" JOHNSON, on meeting her future husband, *Saturday Evening Post,* February 8, 1964

It was an unspoken pleasure, that having come together so many years, ruined so much and repaired a little, we had endured.

> ━ LILLIAN HELLMAN, on her relationship with Dashiell Hammett, recalled on her death, June 30, 1984

It was a very spasmodic courtship, conducted mainly at long distance with a great clanking of coins in dozens of phone booths.

> ━ JACQUELINE KENNEDY ONASSIS, on her romance with John F. Kennedy, in Doris Kearns Goodwin, *The Fitzgeralds and the Kennedys,* 1987

One reason we lasted so long is that we usually played two people who were very much in love. As we were realistic actors, we became those two people. So we had a divertissement: I had an affair with him, and he with me.

> ━ LYNN FONTANNE (1887–1983), U.S. actress, on being married for 55 years to costar Alfred Lunt, in *New York Times,* April 24, 1978

When he's late for dinner, I know he's either having an affair or is lying dead in the street. I always hope it's the street.

> ━ JESSICA TANDY, on her husband Hume Cronyn, Kennedy Center Honors, CBS-TV, December 26, 1986

Wouldn't that be like shoplifting in a secondhand store?

> ━ JEAN HARLOW, when asked if she would steal a husband (1930), in Irving Shulman, *Harlow,* 1964

(*See also* Affairs, Dating, First Love, Free Love, Love, Love Letters, Loving, Mature Love, May-December Romance, Memories of Love, True Love, Unrequited Love)

Farewell

It is never any good dwelling on goodbyes. It is not the being together that it prolongs but the parting.

— ELIZABETH BIBESCO, *The Fir and the Palm,* 1924

In every parting there is the image of death.

— GEORGE ELIOT, *Scenes of Clerical Life,* 1858

In all separations there are the elements of eternity, and in every farewell to the being we love, we set foot upon an undug grave.

— MARY ADAMS, *Confessions of a Wife,* 1902

(*See also* Absence, Alone, Parting)

Fashion

What can you expect of a girl who was allowed to wear black satin at her coming out ball?

— EDITH WHARTON, *The Age of Innocence,* 1920

Look for the woman in the dress. If there is no woman, there is no dress.

— COCO CHANEL, *New York Times,* August 23, 1964

No new fashion worth its salt is ever wearable.

— EUGENIA SHEPPARD, *New York Herald Tribune,* January 13, 1960

The origins of clothing are not practical. They are mystical and erotic. The primitive man in the wolf pelt was not keeping dry; he was saying: Look what I killed. Aren't I the best?

— KATHERINE HAMMETT, *Independent on Sunday,* March 10, 1991

Where's the man could ease a heart like a satin gown?
— DOROTHY PARKER, *The Satin Dress,* 1937

Chanel No. 5.
— MARILYN MONROE, **on being asked what she wore to bed, in Pete Martin's** *Marilyn Monroe,* **1956**

Clothes are our weapons, our challenges, our visible insults.
— ANGELA CARTER, *Nothing Sacred,* 1982

(*See also* Clothes, Elegance, Style)

 *Fathers*

I stopped loving my father a long time ago. What remained was slavery to a pattern.
— ANAÏS NIN, *Under a Glass Bell,* 1944

Down in the bottom of my childhood my father stands laughing.
— TOVE DITLEVSEN, **in Tina Nunnally,** *Early Spring,* **1985**

It doesn't matter who my father was; it matters who I remember he was.
— ANNE SEXTON, *The Poet's Story,* 1972

My father, dead so long now, looms up as unexplored landscape, the mountains of the moon, a text that has lain in a drawer, undeciphered, for which I have had no Rosetta Stone.
— SHIRLEY ABBOTT, *The Bookmaker's Daughter,* 1991

A father had to work only half as hard as any mother to be considered twice as good.
— MARY KAY BLAKELY, *American Mom,* 1994

Fear

Always use the proper name for things. Fear of the name increases fear of the thing itself.
— J. K. ROWLING, *Harry Potter and the Sorcerer's Stone*, 1998

To fear is one thing. To let fear grab you by the tail and swing you around is another.
— KATHERINE PATERSON, *Jacob Have I Loved*, 1980

Fear is a question: what are you afraid of, and why?
— MARILYN FERGUSON, *The Aquarian Conspiracy*, 1980

He who is in the grasp of the cobra can smile at the lightning's forked tongue.
— ALICE TILTON, *Cold Steel*, 1939

The sight of a cage is only frightening to the bird that has once been caught.
— RACHEL FIELD, *All This and Heaven Too*, 1939

Fear is a rabbit on the road, paralyzed in the glare of the headlights. Courage is being the driver.
— BARBARA HOLLAND, *One's Company*, 1992

Feelings

Better to be without logic than without feeling.
— EMILY BRONTË, *The Professor*, 1846

You cannot know what you do not feel.
— MARYA MANNERS, *They*, 1968

Men and women make sad mistakes about their own symptoms, taking their vague uneasy longings, sometimes for genius, sometimes for religion, and oftener still for a mighty love.

⟜ GEORGE ELIOT, *Middlemarch*, 1871

People who cannot feel punish those who do.

⟜ MAY SARTON, *Mrs. Stevens Hears the Mermaids Singing*, 1965

Feminism

"I hate discussions of feminism that end up with who does the dishes," she said. So do I. But at the end, there are always those damned dishes.

⟜ MARILYN FRENCH, *The Women's Room*, 1977

All women are feminists, whether they know it or not.

⟜ ISABELLE HOLLAND, *The Long Search*, 1990

Most women preface their support of the women's movement with "I'm not a feminist, but . . ." But what? You think God is going to get you if you say "I am for women's liberation and . . ." Right?

⟜ VICTORIA BILLINGS, *The Womanbook*, 1974

(*See also* Women's Rights)

Fiction

Fiction is like a spider's web, attached ever so slightly perhaps, but still attached to life at all four corners.

⟜ VIRGINIA WOOLF, *A Room of One's Own*, 1929

Fiction is not a dream. Nor is it guesswork. It is imagining based on facts, and the facts must be accurate or the work of imagining will not stand up.

— MARGARET CULKIN BANNING, *The Writer,* March 1960

First Love

It was first love. There's no love like that. I don't wish it on a soul. I don't hate anyone enough.

— CAROL MATTHAU, *Among the Portuguese,* 1992

It was the kind of desperate, headlong, adolescent calf love that he should have experienced years ago and got over.

— AGATHA CHRISTIE, *Remembered Death,* 1945

I'm glad it cannot happen twice, the fever of first love.

— DAPHNE DU MAURIER, *Rebecca,* 1938

First love is an astounding experience and if the object happens to be totally unworthy and the love not really love at all, it makes little difference to the intensity or the pain.

— ANGELA THIRKELL, *Cheerfulness Breaks In,* 1941

I thought that spring must last forevermore
For I was young and loved, and it was May.

— VERA BRITTAIN, *Poems of the War and After,* 1934

(*See also* Affairs, Dating, Free Love, Love, Love Letters, Love Versus Like, Loving, Memories of Love, True Love, Unrequited Love)

Flattery

The aim of flattery is to soothe and encourage us by assuring us of the truth of an opinion we have already formed about ourselves.
— EDITH SITWELL, *The Last Years of a Rebel,* 1976

Food

A flaccid, moping, debauched mollusk, tired from too much love and loose-nerved from general world conditions, can be a shameful thing served raw upon the shell.
— M. F. K. FISHER, *Consider the Oyster,* 1941

Chocolate is something you have an affair with.
— GENEEN ROTH, *Feeding the Hungry Heart,* 1982

Salad is not a meal. It is a style.
— FRAN LEBOWITZ, *Metropolitan Life,* 1978

A paté is nothing more than a French meat loaf that's had a couple of cocktails.
— CAROL CUTLER, *Paté: The New Main Course for the 80s,* 1983

Truffles must come to the table in their own stock and as you break open this jewel sprung from a poverty-stricken soil, imagine—if you have never visited it—the desolate kingdom where it rules.
— COLETTE, in Maria P. Robbins, *The Cook's Quotation Book,* 1983

Some people *pretend* to like capers, but the truth is that any dish that tastes good with capers in it tastes even better with capers not in it.
— NORA EPHRON, *Heartburn,* 1983

Cocoa. Damn miserable puny stuff, fit for kittens and unwashed boys. Did Shakespeare drink cocoa?

— SHIRLEY JACKSON, *The Bird's Nest,* 1954

If you don't love life, you can't enjoy an oyster.

— ELEANOR CLARK, *The Oysters of Locmariaquer,* 1964

As for butter vs. margarine, I trust cows more than chemists.

— JOAN GUSSOW, *New York Times,* April 16, 1986

For months they have lain in wait, dim shapes lurking in the forgotten corners of houses and factories all over the country and now they are upon us, sodden with alcohol, their massive bodies bulging with strange green protuberances, attacking us in our homes, at our friends' homes, at our offices—there is no escape, it is the hour of the fruitcake.

— DEBORAH PAPIER, "Yeech! The Dreaded Fruitcake!" *Insight,* December 23, 1985

People are tired of going out to expensive restaurants and spending lots of money for seven pea pods and a two-inch steak.

— LYNNE BIEN, *New York Times,* October 3, 1984

In America, even your menus have the gift of language. . . . "The Chef's own Vienna Roast, a hearty, rich meat loaf, gently seasoned to perfection and served in a creamy nest of mashed farm potatoes and strictly fresh garden vegetables." Of course what you get is cole slaw and a slab of meat, but that doesn't matter because the menu has already started your juices going. Oh, those menus. In America, they're poetry.

— LAURIE LEE, *Newsweek,* October 24, 1960

In the childhood memories of every good cook, there's a large kitchen, a warm stove, a simmering pot and a mom.

— BARBARA COSTIKYAN, *New York,* October 22, 1984

(*See also* Coffee, Cooking, Eating, Food, Tea, Wine)

Forgiveness

We can forgive anything as long as it isn't done to us.
— P. D. JAMES, *Innocent Blood*, 1980

Forgiveness is the act of admitting we are like other people.
— CHRISTINA BALDWIN, *Life's Companion*, 1990

Who understands much, forgives much.
— MADAME DE STAËL, *Corrine*, 1807

Freedom

None who have always been free can understand the terrible fascinating power of the hope of freedom to those who are not free.
— PEARL S. BUCK, *What America Means to Me*, 1943

Too much freedom is its own kind of cage.
— PATRICIA MACDONALD, *Secret Admirer*, 1995

Men would rather be starving and free than fed in bonds.
— PEARL S. BUCK, *What America Means to Me*, 1945

Golden fetters hurt as cruelly as iron ones.
— MINNA THOMAS ANTRIM, *Naked Truth and Veiled Allusions*, 1901

Women, like men, ought to have their youth so glutted with freedom they hate the very idea of freedom.
— VITA SACKVILLE-WEST, in letter, June 1, 1919, in *Portrait of a Marriage,* by Nigel Nicolson, 1973

Love will not always linger longest with those who hold it in too clenched a fist.
— ALICE DUER MILLER, *Forsaking All Others*, 1931

Free Love

Free love is too expensive.
— BERNADETTE DEVLIN, *The Price of My Soul,* 1969

(*See also* Affairs, Dating, First Love, Love, Love Letters, Loving, Mature Love, May-December Romance, Memories of Love, Sex, Sex Object, Sexuality, True Love)

Friends

Each friend represents a world in us, a world possibly not born until they arrive, and it is only by this meeting that a new world is born.
— ANAÏS NIN, *The Diary of Anaïs Nin,* 1967

Great friendship is never peaceful.
— MARIE DE RABUTIN-CHANTAL, Marquise de Sévigné, letter to Mme. de Grignan, September 16, 1671

Only solitary men know the full joys of friendship. Others have their family, but to a solitary and an exile, his friends are everything.
— WILLA CATHER, *Shadows on the Rock,* 1931

You can't always be friendly. It's impossible. There isn't time.
— TOVE JANSSON, *Tales From Moominvalley,* 1963

Every murderer is probably somebody's old friend.
— AGATHA CHRISTIE, *The Mysterious Affair at Styles,* 1920

Parents are friends that life gives us; friends are parents that the heart chooses.
— COMTESSE DIANE, *Les Glanes de la Vie,* 1898

Men and women can't be friends because the sex part always gets in the way.
— NORA EPHRON, *When Harry Met Sally,* 1989

In a bad marriage, friends are the invisible glue. If we have enough friends, we may go on for years, intending to leave, talking about leaving—instead of actually getting up and leaving.
— ERICA JONG, *How to Save Your Own Life,* 1977

There will be the year when you buy a bottle of really decent champagne in December because someone worthy of it will surely drop by, and it stays in the refrigerator until March, when you sit down and drink the whole thing yourself and burst into tears.
— BARBARA HOLLAND, *One's Company,* 1922

It is wise to apply the refined oil of politeness to the mechanism of friendship.
— COLETTE, *Earthly Paradise,* 1966

 *Gardening*

A garden isn't meant to be useful. It's for joy.
— RUMER GODDEN, *China Court,* 1961

A garden has a curious innocent way of consuming cash while all the time you are under the illusion that you are spending nothing.
— ESTHER MEYNELL, *A Woman Talking,* 1940

A garden is always a series of losses set against a few triumphs . . .
— MAY SARTON, *At Seventy,* 1984

You must remember that garden catalogues are as big liars as house-agents.
— RUMER GODDEN, *China Court,* 1961

Weather means more when you have a garden.
— MARCELENE COX, in *Ladies' Home Journal*, 1944

Generation Gap

All of us who grew up before the war are immigrants in time, immigrants from an earlier world, living in an age essentially different from anything we knew before. The young are at home here. Their eyes have always seen satellites in the sky. They have never known a world in which war did not mean annihilation.
— MARGARET MEAD, on generation gap of the late 1960s, *Culture and Commitment*, 1970

(*See also* Childhood, Parenting, Youth)

Genius

If it is in you, no cords can confine it.
— GAIL HAMILTON, *Country Living and Country Thinking*, 1862

It is quite hard at times to distinguish a genius from a lunatic.
— DOROTHY THOMPSON, *The Courage to Be Happy*, 1957

God

We need to find God, and He can't be found in noise and restlessness. God is the friend of silence. See how nature—trees, flowers, grass—grows in silence, see the stars, the moon and the sun, how they move in silence. We need silence to be able to touch souls.
— MOTHER TERESA, *A Gift for God*, 1975

My belief is that we did not come from God so much as that we are going toward God.

— JANE DUNCAN, *Letter from Beachfur,* 1975

I distrust those people who know so well what God wants them to do, because I notice it always coincides with their own desires.

— SUSAN B. ANTHONY, convention speech, January 1896, in *Life and Work of Susan B. Anthony* by A. H. Shaw and I. H. Harper, 1902

One needs occasionally to stand aside from the hum and rush of human interests and passions to hear the voices of God.

— ANNA JULIA COOPER, *A Voice in the South,* 1892

God doesn't require us to succeed; He only requires that you try.

— MOTHER TERESA, in *Rolling Stone,* by Robert F. Kennedy, Jr., December 1992

If God exists, I'd be the first to be told.

— ANNA DE NOAILLES, to Jean Cocteau, *Vogue,* May 1984

(*See also* Christianity, Church, Prayer, Religion, Spirituality)

Good Versus Evil

We cannot freely and wisely choose the right way for ourselves unless we know both good and evil.

— HELEN KELLER, *My Religion,* 1927

Gossip

Men have always detested women's gossip because they suspect the truth: their measurements are being taken and compared.

— ERICA JONG, *Fear of Flying,* 1973

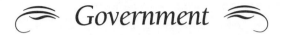

Government

We put up with a lot to be saved from chaos. We always have.
— ELIZABETH JANEWAY, *Improper Behavior,* 1987

Generosity is a virtue for individuals, not governments. When governments are generous it is with other people's money, other people's safety, other people's future.
— P. D. JAMES, *The Children of Men,* 1992

The only people who should be in government are those who care more about people than they do about power.
— MILLICENT FENWICK, *Speaking Up,* 1982

Under a Labour government, there's virtually nowhere you can put your savings where they would be safe from the state. . . . If you put money in a sock, they'd probably nationalize socks.
— MARGARET THATCHER, in *The Downing Street Years,* 1993

A government is not legitimate merely because it exists.
— JEANNE J. KIRKPATRICK, in *Time,* 1985

We must have government, but we must watch them like a hawk.
— MILLICENT FENWICK, in *Reader's Digest,* 1983

Grandparents

Why do grandparents and grandchildren get along so well? They have the same enemy—the mother.
— CLAUDETTE COLBERT, *Time,* September 14, 1981

A home without a grandmother is like an egg without salt.
— FLORENCE KING, *Reflections in a Jaundiced Eye,* 1989

I loved their home. Everything smelled older, worn but safe; the
food aroma had baked itself into the furniture.

— SUSAN STRASBERG, *Bittersweet*, 1980

 *Grief*

Grief can't be shared. Everyone carries it alone, his own burden, his
own way.

— ANNE MORROW LINDBERGH, *Dearly Beloved*, 1962

What's grief but the after-blindness
of the spirit's dazzle of love?

— GWEN HARWOOD, "Past and Present," *Poems*, Volume Two, 1968

Grief is a circular staircase.

— LINDA PASTAN, *The Five Stages of Grief*, 1978

The sun has set in your life; it is getting cold. The hundreds of people around you cannot console you for the loss of the one.

— MARIA VON TRAPP, *The Story of the Trapp Family Singers*, 1949

Sleep brings no joy to me
Remembrance never dies

— EMILY BRONTË, in Clement Shorter, *The Complete Poems of Emily
Brontë*, 1910

 *Growing Up*

A finished person is a boring person.

— ANNA QUINDLEN, in *Writer's Digest*, 1993

All children are lost; their growing is a continuous process of loss. A tall and handsome Emily occasionally strides around the house now, but the little one, with her wispy pigtails and irrational fits of happiness, is as completely gone as if she had walked into the woods one day and never come back.

— BARBARA HOLLAND, *In Private Life*, 1997

Hair

To Crystal, hair was the most important thing on earth. She would never get married because you couldn't wear curlers in bed.

— EDNA O'BRIEN, "Come Into the Drawing Room, Doris," *Winter's Tales 8*, 1962

(*See also* Appearance, Beauty)

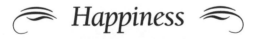

Happiness

The happy ending is our national belief.

— MARY THERESE MCCARTHY, *America the Beautiful*, 1947

When one door of happiness closes, another opens; but often we look so long at the closed door that we do not see the one which has been opened to us.

— HELEN KELLER, *We Bereaved*, 1929

All happiness is a work of art; the smallest error falsifies it, the slightest hesitation alters it, the least heaviness spoils it, the slightest stupidity brutalizes it.

— MARGUERITE YOURCENAR, *Les Mémoires d'Hadrien*, 1951

Adults talk about being happy because largely they are not.
— JEANETTE WINTERSON, *The Passion,* 1987

Happiness should be like an oasis, the greener for the desert that surrounds it.
— RACHEL FIELD, *And Now Tomorrow,* 1942

(*See also* Contentment, Joy)

Hate

I forgave the DAR many years ago. You lose a lot of time hating people.
— MARIAN ANDERSON, **announcing her retirement nearly 25 years after the DAR denied her concert space in Washington, D.C.'s Constitution Hall,** *New York Times,* **December 13, 1963**

I tell you there is such a thing as creative hate.
— WILLA CATHER, *The Song of the Lark,* 1915

Didn't you ever notice how it's always people who wish they had somethin' or had done somethin' that hate the hardest?
— GRACE METALIOUS, *Peyton Place,* 1956

Hate seemed to crackle out of him in little flashes, like electricity in a cat's fur.
— M. F. K. FISHER, *The Gastronomical Me,* 1943

Health Care

It's better to be a pain than a corpse.
— DIANE SACKETT NANNERY, **breast cancer research activist, attributed**

Thousands upon thousands of persons have studied disease. Almost no one has studied health.

➤ ADELE DAVIS, *Let's Eat Right to Keep Fit,* 1954

Heart

Nobody has ever measured, not even poets, how much the heart can hold.

➤ ZELDA FITZGERALD, in Nancy Mitford, *Zelda Fitzgerald: A Biography,* 1970

To wear your heart on your sleeve isn't a very good plan. You should wear it inside, where it functions best.

➤ MARGARET THATCHER, ABC-TV interview, March 18, 1987

The heart of another is a dark forest, always, no matter how close it has been to one's own.

➤ WILLA CATHER, *The Professor's House,* 1925

I know I am but summer to your heart
And not the full four seasons of the year.

➤ EDNA ST. VINCENT MILLAY, "I Know I Am but Summer," *The Harp-Weaver,* 1923

The human heart does not stay away too long from that which hurt it most. There is a return journey to anguish that few of us are released from making.

➤ LILLIAN SMITH, *The Journey,* 1954

(*See also* Affairs, Dating, First Love, Free Love, Heart, Love, Love Versus Like, Love Letters, Loving, Mature Love, May-December Romance, Memories of Love, True Love)

 *Heartbreak*

Pain
rusts into beauty, too
I know full well that this is so:
I had a heartbreak long ago
— MARY CAROLYN DAVIES, "Rust," *Youth Riding,* 1919

A broken heart is what makes life so wonderful five years later, when you see the guy in an elevator and he is fat and smoking a cigar and saying long-time-no-see.
— PHYLLIS BATTELLE, *New York Journal-American,* June 1, 1962

I cannot say what loves have come and gone,
I only know that summer sang in me
A little while, that in me sings no more.
— EDNA ST. VINCENT MILLAY, "**What Lips My Lips Have Kissed, and Where, and Why,**" *The Harp-Weaver,* 1923

Never worry for fear that you have broken a man's heart; at the worst, it is only sprained and a week's rest will put it in perfect working condition again.
— HELEN ROWLAND, *Reflections of a Bachelor Girl,* 1903

where have you gone
with your confident
walk your
crooked smile the
rent money
in one pocket and
my heart in another.
— MARI E. EVANS, "Where Have You Gone," in Dudley Randall (ed) *The Black Poets,* 1971

There are various ways of mending a broken heart, but perhaps going to a learned conference is one of the more unusual.
　— BARBARA PYM, *No Fond Return of Love*, 1961

The time you spend grieving over a man should never exceed the amount of time you actually spent with him.
　— DOROTHY L. SAYERS, *Have His Carcase*, 1932

'Tis not love's going hurts my days
But that it went in little ways.
　— EDNA ST. VINCENT MILLAY, "The Spring and the Fall" *The Harp-Weaver*, 1923

(*See also* Anguish, Betrayal, Divorce, Loneliness, Parting)

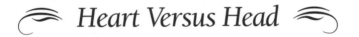

Heart Versus Head

Falling in love consists merely in uncorking the imagination and bottling the common sense.
　— HELEN ROWLAND, "A Guide to Men," *Variations*, 1922

Four be the things I am wiser to know:
Idleness, sorrow, a friend, and a foe.
Four be the things I'd been better without:
Love, curiosity, freckles, and doubt.
　— DOROTHY PARKER, *Enough Rope*, 1927

Never til Time is done
Will the fire of the heart and the fire of the mind be one.
　— EDITH SITWELL, in Elizabeth Salter and Allanah Harper (eds), *Edith Sitwell*, 1976

I am all for people having their heart in the right place, but the right place for a heart is not inside the head.
— KATHARINE WHITEHORN, *Roundabout*, 1962

(*See also* Affairs, Dating, First Love, Free Love, Heart, Love, Love Versus Like, Love Letters, Loving, Mature Love, May-December Romance, Memories of Love, True Love)

History

The sunbonnet as well as the sombrero has helped to settle this glorious land of ours.
— EDNA FERBER, *Cimarron*, 1929

It is sometimes very hard to tell the difference between history and the smell of skunk.
— REBECCA WEST, *Black Lamb and Grey Falcon*, 1941

Not only is history written by the winners, it is also made by them.
— ELIZABETH SCHUSSLER FIORENZA, *In Memory of Her*, 1983

The unrecorded past is none other than our old friend, the tree in the primeval forest which fell without being heard.
— BARBARA TUCHMAN, "Can History Be Served Up Hot?" *New York Times*, March 8, 1964

Home

There are homes you run from, and homes you run to.
— LAURA CUNNINGHAM, *Sleeping Arrangements*, 1989

Don't you know you can't go home again?
— ELLA WINTER, to Thomas Wolfe who asked to use the expression as a book title, 1937

 *Homosexuality*

If you removed all of the homosexuals and homosexual influence from what is generally regarded as American culture, you would be pretty much left with Let's Make a Deal.
— FRAN LEBOWITZ, in *Unnatural Quotations,* 1988

No government has the right to tell its citizens when or whom to love. The only queer people are those who don't love anybody.
— RITA MAE BROWN, speech at the opening ceremony of the Gay Olympics, August 28, 1982

Love is love. Gender is merely spare parts.
— WENDY WASSERSTEIN, *The Sisters Rosenzweig,* 1991

It's funny how heterosexuals have lives and the rest of us have "lifestyles."
— SONIA JOHNSON, *Going Out of Our Minds,* 1987

He was the wren and the rain, he was the wind and the trees bending under the wind. He was split in two, the mover and the moved, the male and the female.
— MARGARET MILLER, *Beast in View,* 1955

It is so true that a woman may be in love with a woman, and a man with a man. It is pleasant to be sure of it, because it is undoubtedly the same love that we shall feel when we are angels.
— MARGARET FULLER, in Mason Wade, *Margaret Fuller, Whetstone of Genius,* 1940

Lesbianism has always seemed to me an extremely inventive response to the shortage of men, but otherwise not worth the trouble.
— NORA EPHRON, *Heartburn,* 1983

(*See also* Bisexuality, Lesbians)

Horses

I still subscribe to the minority view that all horses are offensive weapons and not to be trusted a yard.
— M. M. KAYE, *The Sun in the Morning,* 1990

I do feel that horses have faces—and feelings, too.
— ALANNA KNIGHT, *Lament for Lost Lovers,* 1973

Housework

There is no more fruitful source of family discontent than a housewife's badly-cooked dinner and untidy ways.
— ISABELLA MARY BEETON, *The Book of Household Management,* 1861

Although woman has performed much of the labor of the world, her industry and economy have been the very means of increasing her degradation.
— ELIZABETH CADY STANTON, *The History of Woman Suffrage,* 1881

I think housework is the reason most women go to the office.
— HELOISE (HELOISE CRUSE), *Editor & Publisher,* April 27, 1963

Any woman who understands the problems of running a home will be nearer to understanding the problems of running a country.
— MARGARET THATCHER, interviewed by *The Observer* four days after becoming Britain's first woman Prime Minister, May 8, 1979

The labor of women in the house, certainly, enables men to produce more wealth than they otherwise could; and in this way they are economic factors in society. But so are horses.
— CHARLOTTE ANNA GILMAN, *Women and Economics,* 1898

Human Race

If the whole human race lay in one grave, the epitaph on its head-
stone might well be: "It seemed like a good idea at the time."
— REBECCA WEST, in *The New York Times*, October 2, 1977

Husbands

If you cannot have your dear husband for a comfort and a delight,
for a breadwinner and a crosspatch, for a sofa, chair or a hot-water
bottle, one can use him as a Cross to be Borne.
— STEVIE SMITH, *Novel on Yellow Paper,* 1936

The compulsion to find a husband and lover in a single person has
doomed more women to misery than any other illusion.
— CAROLYN HEILBRUN, *Writing a Woman's Life,* 1988

The only way to make a husband over according to one's
ideas . . . would be to adopt him at an early age . . . say four.
— MARY ROBERTS RINEHART, *Isn't That Just Like a Man,* 1920

If you keep him long enough, he'll come back in style.
— DOROTHY PARKER, **to a woman boasting about her husband of
seven years, in Dorothy Hermann,** *With Malice Toward All,* **1982**

If ever two were one, then surely we.
If ever man were loved by wife, then thee;
If ever wife was happy in a man,
Compare with me ye women if you can.
— ANNE BRADSTREET, *To My Dear and Loving Husband,* 1678

(*See also* Affairs, Dating, First Love, Free Love, Heart, Love, Love
Letters, Loving, Marriage, Mature Love, May-December Romance,
Memories of Love, True Love, Unrequited Love, Wives)

Illness

A man's illness is his private territory and, no matter how much he loves you and how close you are, you stay an outsider. You are healthy.

— LAUREN BACALL, *Lauren Bacall by Myself,* 1979

Now I am beginning to live a little, and feel less like a sick oyster at low tide.

— LOUISA MAY ALCOTT, in *Louisa May Alcott, Her Life, Letters and Journals,* 1890

Apprehension, uncertainty, waiting, expectation, fear of surprise, do a patient more harm than any exertion.

— FLORENCE NIGHTINGALE, *Notes on Nursing,* 1859

Immortality

Memories of our lives, of our works and our deeds will continue in others.

— ROSA PARKS, in "The Meaning of Life," *Life,* December 1988

We were afraid of the dead because we never could tell when they might show up again.

— JAMAICA KINCAID, *Annie John,* 1983

What's so good about a heaven where, one of these days, you're going to get your embarrassing old body back?

— MARSHA NORMAN, *The Fortune Teller,* 1987

Indecision

It is human nature to stand in the middle of a thing.
— MARIANNE MOORE, "A Grave," *Collected Poems,* 1951

Independence

It's easy to be independent when you've got money. But to be independent when you haven't got a thing—that's the Lord's test.
— MAHALIA JACKSON, with Evan McLeod Wylie, *Movin' On Up,* 1966

I dream that love without tyranny is possible.
— ANDREA DWORKIN, "First Love," in Julia Wolf Mazow (ed), *The Woman Who Lost Her Names,* 1980

I leave before being left. I decide.
— BRIGITTE BARDOT, *Newsweek,* March 5, 1973

I have always had a dread of becoming a passenger in life.
— PRINCESS MARGRETHE OF DENMARK, on necessity of independent achievement, *Life,* January 12, 1968

If I'm ever to reach any understanding of myself and the things around me, I must learn to stand alone. That's why I can't stay here with you any longer.
— NORA, in Henrik Ibsen's *A Doll's House,* 1879

I love you so passionately that I hide a great part of my love, not to oppress you with it.
— MARIE DE RABUTIN-CHANTAL, MARQUISE DE SÉVIGNÉ (1671), in *Letters of Mme. de Sévigné to Her Daughter and Her Friends,* vol. 1, 1811

 *Individuality*

Nobody can be exactly like me. Sometimes even I have trouble doing it.
— TALLULAH BANKHEAD, **attributed**

The boughs of no two trees ever have the same arrangement. Nature always produces individuals, she never produces classes.
— LYDIA MARIA CHILD, *Letters From New York*, 1845

The thing that makes you exceptional, if you are at all, is inevitably that which must also make you lonely.
— LORRAINE HANSBERRY, **in Robert Nemiroff,** *To Be Young, Gifted, and Black*, 1969

 *Infidelity*

There are plenty of men who philander during the summer, to be sure, but they are usually the same lot who philander during the winter—albeit with less convenience.
— NORA EPHRON, *New York Post*, **August 22, 1965**

After the door of a woman's heart has once swung on its silent hinges, a man thinks he can prop it open with a brick and go away and leave it.
— MYRTLE REED, *The Spinster Book*, 1901

It is better to be unfaithful than faithful without wanting to be.
— BRIGITTE BARDOT, **"Sayings of the Week,"** *The Observer*, **February 18, 1968**

Love is a boaster at heart, who cannot hide the stolen horse without giving a glimpse of the bridle.

— MARY RENAULT, *The Last of the Wine,* 1956

All I wanted was a man
With a single heart,
. . . Not somebody always after wriggling fish
With his big bamboo rod

— CHUO WEN-CHUN (2nd century B.C.) in Kenneth Rexroth and Ling Chung (eds), THE ORCHID BOAT, 1972

(*See also* Affairs, Dating, First Love, Free Love, Heart, Love, Love Letters, Loving, Mature Love, May-December Romance, Memories of Love, True Love)

Integrity

Integrity is so perishable in the summer months of success.

— VANESSA REDGRAVE, *Goodbye Baby and Amen,* by David Bailey, 1969

Intelligence

A great many people think that polysyllables are a sign of intelligence.

— BARBARA WALTERS, *How to Talk With Practically Anybody About Practically Anything,* 1970

The only sensible answer to the question, "Who is smarter, a man or a woman?" is "Which man and which woman?"

— ESTELLE RAMEY, in Madeline Chinnici, "Do Human Brains Have Gender," *Self,* 1990

 *Ireland*

When anyone asks me about the Irish character, I say look at the trees. Maimed, stark and misshapen, but ferociously tenacious.
— EDNA O'BRIEN, news summaries, December 31, 1965

 *Jealousy*

Jealousy in romance is like salt in food. A little can enhance the savor, but too much can spoil their pleasure and, under certain circumstances, can be life-threatening.
— MAYA ANGELOU, *Wouldn't Take Nothing for My Journey Now,* 1993

To cure jealousy is to see it for what it is, a dissatisfaction with self, an impossible claim that one should be at once Rose Bowl princess, medieval scholar, Saint Joan . . . Eleanor of Aquitaine, one's sister and a stranger in a pink hat seen once and admired on the corner of 55th and Madison—as well as oneself, mysteriously improved.
— JOAN DIDION, "Jealousy: Is It a Curable Illness?" *Vogue,* June 1961

Jealousy had a taste all right. A bitter and tongue-stinging flavor, like a peach pit.
— DOLORES HITCHENS, *In a House Unknown,* 1973

Anger and jealousy can no more bear to lose sight of their objects than love.
— GEORGE ELIOT, *The Mill on the Floss,* 1860

I believe she would be jealous of a fine day if her husband praised it.
— HANNAH MORE, *Coelebs in Search of a Wife,* 1808

The jealous bring down the curse they fear upon their own heads.
— DOROTHY DIX, *Dorothy Dix—Her book,* 1926

Never has jealousy added to character, never does it make the individual big and fine.
— EMMA GOLDMAN, "Jealousy: Causes and a Possible Cure" (1912), in Alix Kates Shulman (ed), *Real Emma Speaks,* 1985

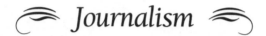

Journalism

The life of the journalist is poor, nasty, brutish and short. So is his style.
— STELLA DOROTHEA GIBBONS, foreword, *Cold Comfort Farm,* 1932

News is like food; it is the cooking and serving that makes it acceptable, not the material itself.
— ROSE MACAULAY, *A Casual Commentary,* 1936

In journalism there has always been a tension between getting it right and getting it first.
— ELLEN GOODMAN, *Boston Globe,* 1993

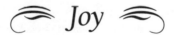

Joy

Joy is fleeting, sinful and the forerunner of despair.
— ALISON KENNEDY, *Looking for the Possible Dance,* 1993

Kisses

First time he kissed me, he but only kissed
The fingers of this hand wherewith I write;
And, ever since, it grew more clean and white.
— ELIZABETH BARRETT BROWNING, *Sonnets from the Portuguese,* 1850

When you kiss me
jaguars lope through my knees
when you kiss me,
my lips quiver like bronze
violets; oh, when you kiss me
— DIANE ACKERMAN, "Beija-Flor," *Jaguar of Sweet Laughter,* 1991

(*See also* Affairs, Dating, First Love, Free Love, Heart, Love, Love
Letters, Loving, Mature Love, May-December Romance, Memories
of Love, Sex, True Love)

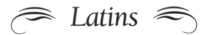

Latins

Latins are tenderly enthusiastic. In Brazil they throw flowers at
you. In Argentina they throw themselves.
— MARLENE DIETRICH, on crowds in Buenos Aires, *Newsweek,*
August 24, 1959

Law

Lawyers [are] operators of the toll bridge across which anyone in
search of justice has to pass.
— JANE BRYANT QUINN, in *Newsweek,* October 9, 1978

I think the law became an ass the day it let the psychiatrists get their hands on it.

> ━ LYNN COMPTON, **chief deputy district attorney, in summation at Sirhan Sirhan's trial for assassination of Robert F. Kennedy,** *L.A. Times,* **April 14, 1969**

Law reform is far too serious a matter to be left to the legal profession.

> ━ LESLIE SCARMAN, **to the New York City Bar Association,** *Record,* **January 1955**

If criminals wanted to grind justice to a halt, they could do it by banding together and all pleading not guilty.

> ━ DOROTHY WRIGHT WILSON, *L.A. Times,* **August 11, 1974**

A lawyer's relationship to justice and wisdom . . . is on a par with a piano tuner's relationship to a concert. He neither composes the music, nor interprets it—he merely keeps the machinery running.

> ━ LUCILLE KALLEN, *Introducing C. B. Greenfield,* **1979**

A lie should be tried in a place where it will attract the attention of the world.

> ━ ARIEL SHARON, **on bringing libel suit against** *Time* **magazine,** *The New York Times,* **November 20, 1984**

Leadership

You cannot manage men into battle. You manage things; you lead people.

> ━ GRACE MURRAY HOPPER, **on** *Nova,* **PBS-TV, 1986**

Lesbians

Are there many things in this cool-hearted world so utterly exquisite as the pure love of one woman for another woman?
— MARY MACLANE, *The Story of Mary MacLane*, 1902

I will be quiet, be still, and know that it is God who put the love for women in my heart.
— BRIGITTE ROBERTS, "Be Still and Know," in Naomi Holoch and Joan Nestle (eds), *Women on Women*, 1993

A woman
who loves a woman
is forever young
— ANNE SEXTON, "Rapunzel," *Transformations*, 1971

(*See also* Bisexuality, Homosexuality)

Lies

It was not the man I deceived the most that I loved the most.
— MARGUERITE DURAS, *Practicalities*, 1990

(*See also* Betrayal)

Life

Why is life speeded up so? Why are things so terribly, unbearably precious that you can't enjoy them but can only wait breathless in dread of their going?
— ANNE MORROW LINDBERGH, *Hour of Gold, Hour of Lead*, 1973

Life loves the liver of it.
— MAYA ANGELOU, in *Conversations with Maya Angelou,* 1989

Life is too short to stuff a mushroom.
— SHIRLEY CONRAN, *Superwoman,* 1975

The thousands of possible lives that used to spread out in front of me have snapped shut into one, and all I get is what I've got. It's time to pass on the possibilities, all those deliciously half-open doors, to my children, and drive them to airports, and wish them bon voyage.
— BARBARA HOLLAND, *In Private Life,* 1997

Life ought to be a struggle of desire toward adventures whose nobility will fertilize the soul.
— REBECCA WEST, in *Glimpses of the Great,* by A. L. Rowse, 1986

Life itself is the proper binge.
— JULIA CHILD, *Time,* January 7, 1980

If I had my life to live over, I would have eaten popcorn in the "good" living room and worried much less about the dirt when someone wanted to make a fire in the fireplace.
— ERMA BOMBECK, column

In the life of each of us, I said to myself, there is a place remote and islanded, and given to endless regret or secret happiness.
— SARAH ORNE JEWETT, *The Country of the Pointed Firs,* 1896

I like living. I have sometimes been wildly, despairingly, acutely miserable, racked with sorrow, but through it all I still know quite certainly that just to be alive is a grand thing.
— AGATHA CHRISTIE, *An Autobiography,* 1977

Life is either a daring adventure, or nothing. . . . Security is mostly a superstition. It does not exist in nature.
— HELEN KELLER, *The Open Door,* 1957

Life was meant to be lived, and curiosity must be kept alive. One must never, for whatever reason, turn his back on life.

— ELEANOR ROOSEVELT, *Autobiography of Eleanor Roosevelt,* 1961

It's all been very interesting.

— LADY MARY WORTLEY MONTAGU, *last words,* 1762

It's life, isn't it? You plow ahead and make a hit. And you plow on and someone passes you. Then someone passes them. Time levels.

— KATHARINE HEPBURN, *A Remarkable Woman,* by Anne Edwards, 1985

Life forms illogical patterns. It is haphazard and full of beauties which I try to catch as they fly by, for who knows whether any of them will ever return?

— MARGOT FONTEYN, *Margot Fonteyn,* 1976

Life does not accommodate you, it shatters you. It is meant to, and it couldn't do it better. Every seed destroys its container or else there would be no fruition.

— FLORIDA SCOTT-MAXWELL, *The Measure of My Days,* 1968

Life is a succession of moments,
To live each one is to succeed.

— CORITA KENT, *Newsweek,* December 17, 1984

 *Lists*

Lists multiply at a fairly constant rate most of the time, but they do have special breeding seasons when they simply burst into fertility, like fleas.

— BARBARA HOLLAND, *In Private Life,* 1997

Literature

Literature . . . is lonely and waited for, brilliant and pure and frightened, a marriage of birds, a conversation of the blind.
— LORRIE MOORE, *The New York Times,* July 10, 1988

I'm interested in the Gothic novel because it's very much a woman's form. Why is there such wide readership for books that essentially say, "Your husband is trying to kill you"?
— MARGARET ATWOOD, *Margaret Atwood: Conversations,* 1990

Loneliness

You can live a lifetime and at the end of it, know more about other people than you know about yourself. You learn to watch other people, but you never watch yourself because you strive against loneliness. If you read a book, or shuffle a deck of cards, or care for a dog, you're avoiding yourself.
— BERYL MARKHAM, *West with the Night,* 1983

Many a housewife staring at the back of her husband's newspaper, or listening to his breathing in bed is lonelier than any spinster in a rented room.
— GERMAINE GREER, *The Female Eunuch,* 1970

Love all the people you can. The sufferings from love are not to be compared to the sorrows of loneliness.
— SUSAN HALE (1868), in Caroline P. Atkinson (ed), *Letters of Susan Hale,* 1918

Lonely people talking to each other can make each other lonelier.
— LILLIAN HELLMAN, *The Autumn Garden,* 1951

Courage is the price that life exacts for granting peace.
The soul that knows it not, knows no release
From little things:
Knows not the livid loneliness of fear.

— AMELIA EARHART, *Courage*, 1937

(*See also* Absence, Alone, Farewell, Parting)

Longing

Is there anything better than to be longing for something, when you know it is within reach?

— GRETA GARBO, in *The Divine Garbo*, by Frederick Sands and Sven Broman, 1979

Love

But love me for love's sake, that evermore thou may'st love on through love's eternity.

— ELIZABETH BARRETT BROWNING, *Sonnets from the Portuguese*, 1850

Mortal love is but the licking of honey from thorns.

— ANONYMOUS WOMAN at the court of Eleanor of Aquitaine (1198), in Helen Lawrenson, *Whistling Girl*, 1978

The one certain way for a woman to hold a man is to leave him for religion.

— DAME MURIEL SARAH SPARK, *The Comforters*, 1957

If it is your time love will track you down like a cruise missile. If you say "No! I don't want it right now," that's when you'll get it for sure.

— LYNDA BARRY, *Big Ideas*, 1983

He would have fallen in love with me, I think, if I had been built like
Brunhilde and had a mustache and the mind of an Easter chick.

— ANNE RIVERS SIDDONS, *Hill Towns,* 1993

When first we fall in love, we feel that we know all there is to know
about life. And perhaps we are right.

— MIGNON MCLAUGHLIN, *The Neurotic's Notebook,* 1963

To fall in love you have to be in the state of mind for it to take, like
a disease.

— NANCY MITFORD, in *Uncommon Scold,* by Abby Adams, 1989

Whoever has loved knows all that life contains of sorrow and of joy.

— GEORGE SAND, in *French Wit and Wisdom,* 1950

One hour of right-down love
Is worth an age of dully living on.

— APHRA BEHN, in *Uncommon Scold,* by Abby Adams, 1989

To be half of a loving couple is a great source of joy and strength for
humans . . . but looking around among our friends and relations
we can see that it's not that common.

— BARBARA HOLLAND, *One's Company,* 1992

I believe in the curative powers of love as the English believe in tea
or Catholics believe in the Miracle of Lourdes.

— JOYCE JOHNSON, *Minor Characters,* 1983

I always wanted to be in love, always. It's like being a tuning fork.

— EDNA O'BRIEN, "Diary of an Unfaithful Wife," in *Cosmopolitan,*
1966

Whoso loves
Believes the impossible

— ELIZABETH BARRETT BROWNING, *Aurora Leigh,* 1857

It is the same in love as in war; a fortress that parleys is half taken.
— MARGUERITE DE VALOIS, *Memoirs*, 1920

People talk about love as though it were something you could give,
like an armful of flowers. And a lot of people give love like that—
just dump it down on top of you, a useless strong-scented burden.
— ANNE MORROW LINDBERGH, *Locked Rooms and Open Doors*, 1974

I guess what everyone wants more than anything else is to be loved.
— ELLA FITZGERALD, in *Newsweek*, June 7, 1954

Love doesn't just sit there, like a stone, it has to be made, like bread;
remade all the time, made new.
— URSULA LE GUIN, *The Lathe of Heaven*, 1971

Two persons love in one another the future good which they aid
one another to unfold.
— MARGARET FULLER, *Women in the Ninteenth Century*, 1845

Life in common among people who love each other is the ideal of
happiness.
— GEORGE SAND, *Histoire de Ma Vie*, 1856

How do I love thee? Let me count the ways.
I love thee to the depth and breadth and height
My soul can reach, when feeling out of sight
For the ends of Being and ideal Grace.
— ELIZABETH BARRETT BROWNING, *Sonnets from the Portuguese*, 1850

Great loves too must be endured.
— COCO CHANEL, in Marcel Baedrich, *Coco Chanel*, 1972

It was a great holiness, a religion, as all great loves must be.
— ELSIE DE WOLFE, *After all*, 1935

Great loves were almost always great tragedies. Perhaps it was because love was never truly great until the element of sacrifice entered into it.

━ MARY ROBERTS RINEHART, *Dangerous Days*, 1919

In a great romance, each person basically plays a part that the other really likes.

━ ELIZABETH ASHLEY, in *The San Francisco Chronicle*, 1982

There is only one happiness in life: to love and be loved.

━ GEORGE SAND, letter to Lina Calamatta, March 31, 1862

Love is much nicer to be in than an automobile accident, a tight girdle, a higher tax bracket or a holding pattern over Philadelphia.

━ JUDITH VIORST, in *Redbook*, 1975

Love's a thin diet, nor will keep out cold.

━ APHRA BEHN, *The Lucky Chance*, 1686

We love what we would scorn if we were wiser.

━ MARIE DE FRANCE (12th century), in Jeanette Beer, *Medieval Fables of Marie de France*, 1981

A woman has got to love a bad man once or twice in her life, to be thankful for a good one.

━ MARJORIE KINNAN RAWLINGS, *The Yearling*, 1938

Love is a force. It is not a result; it is a cause. It is not a product; it produces. It is a power, like money or steam or electricity.

━ ANNE MORROW LINDBERGH, *Locked Rooms and Open Doors*, 1974

Love has the quality of informing almost everything—even one's work.

━ SYLVIA ASHTON-WARNER, *Myself*, 1967

The fate of love is that it always sees too little or too much.
—— AMELIA BARR, *The Belle of Bolling Green,* 1904

The mind I love must have wild places, a tangled orchard where dark damsons drop in the heavy grass, an overgrown little wood, the chance of a snake or two, a pool that nobody's fathomed the depth of, and paths threaded with flowers planted by the mind.
—— KATHERINE MANSFIELD, *Journal of Katherine Mansfield,* 1927

If thou must love me, let it be for naught
Except for love's sake only.
—— ELIZABETH BARRETT BROWNING, *Sonnets from the Portuguese,* 1850

I am Heathcliff—he's always, always in my mind—not as a plea-sure, any more than I am always a pleasure to myself—but as my own being.
—— CATHERINE EARNSHAW in *Wuthering Heights,* by Emily Brontë, 1847

The world has little to bestow
Where two fond hearts in equal love are joined.
—— ANNIE LAETITIA BARBAULD, "Delia" (1773), *The Works of Anna Laetitia Barbauld,* vol. 1, 1825

We love because it's the only true adventure.
—— NIKKI GIOVANNI, *Reader's Digest,* 1982

Love is not enough. It must be the foundation, the cornerstone, but not the complete structure. It is much too pliable, too yielding.
—— BETTE DAVIS, *The Lonely Life,* 1962

It was a love like a chord from Bach
of such pure gravity.
—— NINA CASSIAN, "It Was a Love" (1963), *Call Yourself Alive?* 1988

We love as soon as we learn to distinguish a separate "you" and "me." Love is our attempt to assuage the terror and isolation of that separateness.
—— JUDITH VIORST, *Necessary Losses,* 1986

Love is a context, not a behavior.
— MARILYN FERGUSON, *The Careen Conspiracy,* 1980

Love is a fruit in season all the time.
— MOTHER TERESA, *A Gift for God,* 1975

Love is a wound within the body
That has no outward sign.
— MARIE DE FRANCE, "Love is a wound within the body," 1981

I have found the paradox that if I love until it hurts, then there is no hurt, but only more love.
— DAPHNE RAE, *Love Until It Hurts,* 1980

The pain of love is the pain of being alive. It's a perpetual wound.
— MAUREEN DUFFY, *Wounds,* 1969

I am not sure at all
if love is salve
or just
a deeper kind of wound
I do not think it matters
— ERICA JONG, "The Evidence," *Half-Lives,* 1971

Sometimes idiosyncrasies which used to be irritating become endearing, part of the complexity of a partner who has become woven deep into our own selves.
— MADELEINE L'ENGLE, *Two-Part Invention,* 1988

Even when the first wild desire is gone, especially then, there is an inherent need for good manners and consideration, for the putting forth of effort. Two courteous and civilized human beings out of the loneliness of their souls owe that to each other.
— ILKA CHASE, *In Bed We Cry,* 1943

True love isn't the kind that endures through long years of absence, but the kind that endures through long years of propinquity.
— HELEN ROWLAND, *A Guide to Men,* 1922

I wonder why love is so often equated with joy when it is everything else as well. Devastation, balm, obsession, granting and receiving excessive value, and losing it again. It is recognition, often of what you are not but might be. It scars and it heals, it is beyond pity and above law. It can seem like truth.

➤ FLORIDA SCOT-MAXWELL, *The Measure of My Days,* 1968

(*See also* Affairs, Dating, First Love, Free Love, Heart, Love versus Hate, Love versus Like, Love Letters, Loving, Mature Love, May-December Romance, Memories of Love, True Love, Unrequited Love, Young Love)

Love at First Sight

The advantage of love at first sight is that it delays a second sight.

➤ NATALIE CLIFFORD BARNEY, in "Adam," *Samples from Almost Illegible Notebooks,* 1962

(*See also* First Love, Free Love, Love, Loving, Mature Love, May-December Romance, Memories of Love, True Love, Unrequited Love)

Love Letters

There's no finer caress than a love letter, because it makes the world very small, and the writer and reader the only rulers.

➤ CECILIA CAPUZZI, in Octavia Capuzzi Locke, *Johns Hopkins Magazine,* 1987

(*See also* First Love, Free Love, Love, Loving, Mature Love, May-December Romance, Memories of Love, True Love, Unrequited Love)

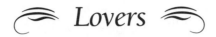

Lovers

Secretly, we wish that anyone we love will think exactly the way we do.
— KIM CHERNIN, *In My Mother's House,* 1983

I am not at all the sort of person you and I took me for.
— JANE CARLYLE, letter to Thomas Carlyle, May 7, 1822

Him that I love, I wish to be free
Even from me
— ANNE MORROW LINDBERGH, "Even," *The Unicorn,* 1956

He's more myself than I am. Whatever our souls are made of his and mine are the same.
— EMILY BRONTË, *Wuthering Heights,* 1847

(*See also* First Love, Free Love, Love, Love at First Sight, Love Letters, Love Versus Hate, Love Versus Like, Loving, Mature Love, May-December Romance, Memories of Love, True Love, Unrequited Love)

Love Versus Hate

Love lights more fires than hate extinguishes.
— ELLA WHEELER WILCOX, "Optimism," *Poems of Pleasure,* 1888

We fluctuate long between love and hatred before we can arrive at tranquility.
— HÉLOÏSE, first letter to Abelard, c. 1122

Hatred is a passion requiring one hundred times the energy of love. Keep it for a cause, not an individual.

— OLIVE MOORE, *Collected Writings*, 1992

(*See also* First Love, Free Love, Love, Love at First Sight, Love Versus Like, Loving, Mature Love, May-December Romance, Memories of Love, True Love, Unrequited Love)

Love Versus Like

Love is like the wild rose-briar; friendship like the holly-tree. The holly is dark when the rose-briar blooms, but which will bloom most constantly?

— EMILY BRONTË, *Love and Friendship*, 1839

The end
of passion
may refashion
a friend

— MONA VAN DUYN, "The Beginning," *Firefall*, 1993

Love is the same as like except you feel sexier.

— JUDITH VIORST, *Love and Guilt and the Meaning of Life, Etc.*, 1979

(*See also* First Love, Free Love, Love, Love at First Sight, Love Versus Hate, Loving, Marriage, Mature Love, May-December Romance, Memories of Love, True Love, Unrequited Love)

Loving

The story of a love is not important—what is important is that one is capable of love. It's perhaps the only glimpse we are permitted of eternity.

    — Helen Hayes, *Guideposts,* January 1960

I have drunk of the wine of life at last, I have known the thing best worth knowing, I have been warmed through and through, never to grow quite cold again til the end.

    — Edith Wharton (1908), in Gloria C. Erlich, *The Sexual Education of Edith Wharton,* 1992

Accustom yourself continually to make many acts of love, for they enkindle and melt the soul.

    — St. Teresa of Avila, "Maxims for Her Nuns," in *Selected Writings of St. Teresa of Avila,* edited by E. Allison Peers, William J. Doheny, 1950

I have no patience with women who measure and weigh their love like a country doctor dispensing capsules. If a man is worth loving at all, he is worth loving generously, even recklessly.

    — Marie Dressler, *The Life Story of an Ugly Duckling,* 1924

(*See also* First Love, Free Love, Love, Love at First Sight, Love Letters, Love Versus Hate, Love Versus Like, Mature Love, May-December Romance, Memories of Love, True Love, Unrequited Love)

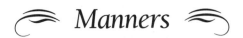

Manners

The gentle and respectful ways of saying "To hell with you" are being abandoned.

    — Millicent Fenwick, recalled on her death, September 16, 1993

When a society abandons its ideals just because most people can't live up to them, behavior gets very ugly indeed.

— JUDITH MARTIN, *Miss Manners' Guide to Rearing Perfect Children,* 1997

Being offended is the natural consequence of leaving one's home.

— FRAN LEBOWITZ, *Social Studies,* 1981

 *Marriage*

All these revered gentlemen who insist on the word "obey" in the marriage service should be removed for a clear violation of the Thirteenth Amendment to the federal Constitution, which says there shall be neither slavery nor involuntary servitude within the United States.

— ELIZABETH CADY STANTON, *Eighty Years and More* (1889)

One of the differences between marriage and prostitution is that in marriage you only have to make a deal with one man.

— ANDREA DWORKIN, *The A.B.C.s of Reading,* 1984

The deep, deep peace of the double-bed after the hurly-burly of the chaise lounge.

— MRS. PATRICK CAMPBELL, in *While Rome Burns,* 1934

If marriage is such a blessed state, how comes it may you say, that there are so few happy marriages?

— MARY ASTELL, *Some Reflections Upon Marriage,* 1706

I wonder what Adam and Eve think of it by this time.

— MARIANNE MOORE, 1935

Marriage, to women as to men, must be a luxury, not a necessity; an incident of life, not all of it. And the only possible way to accomplish this great change is to accord to women equal power in the making, shaping and controlling of the circumstances of life.

— SUSAN B. ANTHONY, Speech on Social Parity, Spring 1875

Life is too short to waste on the admiration of one man.

— ROSE SCOTT, her response to offers of marriage quoted in Jennifer Uglow, *The Macmillan Dictionary of Women's Biography,* 1989

One advantage of marriage, it seems to me, is that when you fall out of love with him, or he falls out of love with you, it keeps you together until you maybe fall in again.

— JUDITH VIORST, "What Is This Thing Called Love?" *Redbook,* February 1975

What a holler would ensue if people had to pay the minister as much to marry them as they have to pay a lawyer to get them a divorce.

— CLAIRE TREVOR, *New York Journal-American,* October 12, 1960

Never marry a man who hates his mother, because he'll end up hating you.

— JILL BENNETT, *Observer,* September 12, 1982

It takes a long time to be really married. One marries many times at many levels within a marriage. If you have more marriages than you have divorces within the marriage, you're lucky and you stick it out.

— RUBY DEE, in Brian Lanker, *I Dream a World,* 1989

Perhaps loving something is the only starting place there is for making your life your own.

— ALICE KOLLER, *An Unknown Woman,* 1982

Look for a sweet person. Forget rich.

— ESTÉE LAUDER, advice on choosing a spouse, in *The New Yorker,* September 15, 1986

To keep the fire burning brightly there's one easy rule: Keep the two logs together, near enough to keep each other warm and far enough apart—about a finger's breadth—for breathing room. Good fire, good marriage, same rule.

➤ MARNIE REED CROWELL, *Greener Pastures,* 1973

There is probably nothing like living together for blinding people to each other.

➤ IVY COMPTON-BURNETT, in *Uncommon Scold,* by Abby Adams, 1989

Marriage is a series of desperate arguments people feel passionately about.

➤ KATHARINE HEPBURN, *Kate,* 1975

Take each other for better or worse, but not for granted.

➤ ARLENE DAHL, *Always Ask a Man,* 1965

I suspect that in every good marriage there are times when love seems to be over.

➤ MADELEINE L'ENGLE, *Two-Part Invention,* 1988

(*See also* Affairs, Divorce, First Love, Free Love, Husbands, Infidelity, Love, Love at First Sight, Loving, Mature Love, May-December Romance, Memories of Love, Mothers-in-Law, True Love, Wedding, Wives)

Mature Love

Summer days are over!
O my one true lover
Sit we now alone together
In the early autumn weather!
From our nest the birds have flown
To fair dreamlands of their own
And we see the days go by
In silence—thou and I!

➤ JULIA C. R. DORR, "Thou and I," *Poems,* 1892

You see I thought love got easier over the years so it didn't hurt so bad when it hurt, or feel so good when it felt good. I thought it smoothed out and old people hardly noticed it. I thought it curled up and died, I guess. Now I saw it rear up like a whip and lash.

—— LOUISE ERDRICH, *Love Medicine,* 1984

(*See also* Age, Love, Love at First Sight, Love Letters, Loving, May-December Romance, Memories of Love, True Love)

 ## *May-December Romance*

How absurd and delicious it is to be in love with somebody younger than yourself! Everybody should try it.

—— BARBARA PYM (1938), in Hazel Holt, *A Lot to Ask,* 1990

(*See also* Affairs, First Love, Free Love, Love, Love at First Sight, Love Letters, Loving, Memories of Love, True Love)

 ## *Memories*

What a strange thing is memory, and hope; one looks backward, the other forward; one is of today, the other of tomorrow.

—— GRANDMA MOSES, *My Life's History,* edited by Aotto Kallir

All you can really do is remember. The present zips by pretty quickly, but the past hangs around. You see it better backward; you can see the children, all of them, the children they were every winter and summer, in the different coats and bathing suits they wore, and watch them all walk into the woods and never come back.

—— BARBARA HOLLAND, *In Private Life,* 1997

Memories of Love

Memory is to love what the saucer is to the cup.
— ELIZABETH BOWEN, *The House in Paris,* 1935

Women and elephants never forget.
— DOROTHY PARKER, *Death and Taxes,* 1931

(*See also* Age, Memory)

Men

When you call upon a Thoroughbred, he gives you all the speed, strength of heart and sinew in him. When you call on a jackass, he kicks.
— PATRICIA NEAL, *As I Am: An Autobiography,* 1988

Remember, all men would be tyrants if they could.
— ABIGAIL ADAMS, letter to John Adams, March 31, 1776

Men are very fragile creatures. Their psyches are so closely tied to their epididymis.
— BETTE STEPHENSON, *Globe and Mail,* July 12, 1975

I don't hate men, I just wish they'd try harder. They all want to be heroes and all we want is for them to stay at home and help with the housework and the kids. That's not the kind of heroism they enjoy.
— JEANETTE WINTERSON, *Sexing the Cherry,* 1989

Bloody men are like bloody buses
You wait for about a year
And as soon as one approaches your stop
Two or three others appear
— WENDY COPE, *Serious Concerns,* 1992

His dominance is not that of one chosen as best fitted to rule . . . but it is sovereignty based on the accident of sex.
— CHARLOTTE ANNA GILMAN, *Women and Economics,* 1898

The man who treasures his friends is usually solid gold himself.
— MARJORIE HOLMES, *Love and Laughter,* 1967

Love is like playing checkers. You have to know which man to move.
— JACKIE "MOMS" MABLEY, interview in *Black Stars,* May 1973

It's not the men in my life that counts, it's the life in my men.
— MAE WEST, in *Diamond Lil,* 1932

It takes a woman 20 years to make a man of her son, and another woman 20 minutes to make a fool of him.
— HELEN ROWLAND, *Reflections of a Bachelor Girl,* 1903

Men weren't really the enemy—they were fellow victims suffering from an outmoded masculine mystique that made them feel unnecessarily inadequate when there were no bears to kill.
— BETTY FRIEDAN, *Christian Science Monitor,* April 1974

I love men, not because they are men, but because they are not women.
— CHRISTINA OF SWEDEN, "Maxims, 1660–1680," in *Pensées de Christine, Reine de Suède,* 1825

Can you imagine a world without men? No crime and lots of fat, happy women.
— NICOLE HOLLANDER, *Sylvia,* 1981

Do you know why God withheld the sense of humour from women? That we may love you instead of laughing at you.
— MRS. PATRICK CAMPBELL, "To a Man," in *Mrs. Pat: The Life of Mrs. Pat Campbell,* by M. Peters, 1984

You have to be very fond of men. Very, very fond. You have to be very fond of them to love them. Otherwise, they're simply unbearable.
— MARGUERITE DURAS, *Practicalities,* 1987

(*See also* Husbands, Women Versus Men)

 Misery

Misery is when you make your bed and then your mother tells you it's the day she's changing the sheets.
— SUZANNE HELLER, *Misery,* 1964

 Mistakes

There are no mistakes, no coincidences. All events are blessings given to us to learn from.
— ELISABETH KÜBLER-ROSS, in *Yoga Journal,* November 1, 1976

 Money

Some women won't buy anything unless they can pay a lot.
— HELENA RUBENSTEIN, in *Time,* April 9, 1965

Brass shines as fair to the ignorant as gold to the goldsmiths.
— ELIZABETH I, letter, 1581

The shortest recorded period of time lies between the minute you put some money away for a rainy day and the unexpected arrival of rain.
— JANE BRYANT QUINN, **Washington Post Writer's Group**

As much money and life as you could want—the two things most human beings would choose above all. The trouble is that humans do have a knack for choosing precisely those things that are worst for them.

➤ J. K. Rowling, *Harry Potter and the Sorcerer's Stone*, 1998

Pennies do not come from heaven. They have to be earned here on earth.

➤ Margaret Thatcher, *Sunday Telegraph*, 1980

 **Morality**

People are very inclined to set moral standards for others.

➤ Elizabeth Drew, *The New Yorker*, February 16, 1987

 **Morals**

There's no such thing as a moral dress. It's people who are moral or immoral.

➤ Jeanette Churchill, "That Moral Dress," in the *Daily Chronicle*, February 16, 1921

 **Mothers**

A mother is never cocky nor proud, because she knows the school principal may call at any minute to report that her child has just driven a motorcycle through the gymnasium.

➤ Mary Kay Blakely, "The Pros and Cons of Motherhood," in Gloria Kaufman and Mary Kay Blakely (eds), *Pulling Our Own Strings*, 1980

Motherhood will only be a joyous and responsible human act when women are free to make, with full conscious choice and full human responsibility, the decisions to become mothers.

— BETTY FRIEDAN, speech at First National Conference for Repeal of Abortion Laws, Chicago, 1969

No song or poem will bear my mother's name. Yet so many of the stories that I write, that we all write, are my mother's stories.

— ALICE WALKER, title essay (1974), in *In Search of Our Mothers' Gardens*, 1983

No matter how old a mother is, she watches her middle-aged children for signs of improvement.

— FLORIDA SCOTT-MAXWELL, *The Measure of My Days*, 1968

I love my mother, not as a prisoner of atherosclerosis, but as a person; and I must love her enough to accept her as she is, now, for as long as this dwindling may take.

— MADELEINE L'ENGLE, *The Summer of the Great-Grandmother*, 1974

A mother's love for her child is like nothing else in the world. It knows no law, no pity, it dares all things and crushes down remorselessly all that stands in its path.

— AGATHA CHRISTIE, "The Last Seance," *The Hound of Death*, 1933

My mother, religious-negro, proud of
having waded through a storm, is very obviously,
a sturdy Black bridge that I
crossed over, on.

— CAROLYN M. RODGERS, "It is deep (don't never forget the bridge that you crossed over on)," *How I Got Ovah*, 1975

You never get over bein' a child long's you have a mother to go to.

— SARAH ORNE JEWETT, *The Country of the Pointed Firs*, 1896

I want to lean into her the way wheat leans into the wind.

— LOUISE ERDRICH, *The Beet Queen*, 1986

treetalk and windsong are
the language of my mother
her music does not leave me.
— BARBARA MAHONE, title poem, *Sugarfield*, 1970

To her whose heart is my heart's quiet home,
To my first Love, my Mother, on whose knee
I learnt love-lore that is not troublesome.
— CHRISTINA ROSSETTI, "Sonnets Are Full of Love," *A Pageant*, 1881

Motherhood is like Albania—you can't trust the descriptions in the books, you have to go there.
— MARNI JACKSON, *The Mother Zone*, 1992

Yes, Mother. I can see you are flawed. You have not hidden it. That is your greatest gift to me.
— ALICE WALKER, *Possessing the Secret of Joy*, 1992

To describe my mother would be to write about a hurricane in its perfect power.
— MAYA ANGELOU, *I Know Why the Caged Bird Sings*, 1970

If you believe in the maternal instinct and fail at mother love, you fail as a woman. It is a controlling idea that holds us in an iron grip.
— NANCY FRIDAY, *My Mother, My Self*, 1977

We want . . . someone to take the intense personal interest in our physical condition that no one else ever has or ever will, and that probably irritated us into tantrums, back in the days of being mothered.
— BARBARA HOLLAND, *One's Company*, 1992

(*See also* Babies; Blame; Childbirth; Childhood; Children; Daughters; Family; Fathers; Mothers and Sons; Mothers-Daughters; Mothers, Death of; Parenting; Wives)

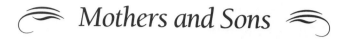

Mothers and Sons

The tie is stronger than that between father and son and father and daughter. . . . The bond is also more complex than the one between mother and daughter. For a woman, a son offers the best chance to know the mysterious male existence.

—CAROLE KLEIN, *Mothers and Sons,* 1984

(*See also* Adolescence, Childhood, Children, Daughters, Family, Fathers, Mothers-Daughters, Parenting, Teenagers)

Mothers-Daughters

A woman *is* her mother. That's the main thing.

—ANNE SEXTON, "Housewife," *All My Pretty Ones,* 1961

Always that tyrannical love reaches out. Soft words shrivel me like quicklime. She will not allow me to be cold, hungry. She will insist that I take her own coat, her own food.

—ELIZABETH SMART, "Dig a Grave and Let Us Bury Our Mother," 1939

I am a reflection of my mother's secret poetry as well as of her hidden angers.

—AUDRE LORDE, *Zami: A New Spelling of My Name,* 1982

In search of my mother's garden, I found my own.

—ALICE WALKER, title essay (1974), *In Search of Our Mothers' Gardens,* 1983

I . . . have another cup of coffee with my mother. We get along very well, veterans of a guerrilla war we never understood.

—JOAN DIDION, "On Going Home," *Slouching Towards Bethlehem,* 1968

My mother and I could always look out the same window without ever seeing the same thing.
— GLORIA SWANSON, *Swanson on Swanson*, 1980

Whenever I'm with my mother, I feel as though I have to spend the whole time avoiding land mines.
— AMY TAN, *The Kitchen God's Wife*, 1991

What I object to in Mother is that she wants me to think her thoughts. Apart from the question of hypocrisy, I prefer my own.
— MARGARET DELAND, *The Rising Tide*, 1916

I fear, as any daughter would, losing myself back into the mother.
— KIM CHERNIN, *In My Mother's House*, 1983

 *Mothers, Death of*

I feel about mothers the way I feel about dimples; because I don't have one myself, I notice everyone who does.
— LETTY COTTIN POGREBIN, *Deborah, Golda and Me*, 1991

I grow old, old
without you, Mother, landscape
of my heart
— OLGA BROUMAS, "Little Red Riding Hood," *Beginning with O*, 1977

We buried her . . . this mother with whom I fought so desperately, whom I loved so dearly, and of whose presence I grow daily more and more conscious.
— ETHEL SMYTH, *Impressions That Remained*, 1919

Inside my mother's death
I lay and could not breathe.
— MAY SARTON, "Dream," *The Silence Now*, 1988

My mother was dead for five years before I knew that I had loved her very much.

— LILLIAN HELLMAN, *An Unfinished Woman,* 1969

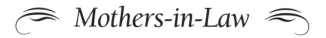

Mothers-in-Law

Of all the peoples whom I have studied, from city dwellers to cliff dwellers, I always find that at least 50% would prefer to have at least one jungle between themselves and their mothers-in-law.

— MARGARET MEAD, **recalled on her death, November 15, 1978**

Movies

Adding sound to movies would be like putting lipstick on the Venus de Milo.

— MARY PICKFORD, **recalled on her death, May 29, 1979**

Music

Do not take up music unless you would rather die than not do so.

— NADIA BOULANGER, **advice to her pupils,** *The Tender Tyrant Nadia Boulanger,* 1976

I wish the government would put a tax on pianos for the incompetent.

— DAME EDITH SITWELL, *Letters 1916–1964,* 1970

Music is a gift and a burden I've had since I can remember who I was. I was born into music. The decision was how to make the best use of it.

— NINA SIMONE, **quoted in Art Taylor,** *Notes and Tones,* 1977

I never practice; I always play.
— WANDA LANDOWSKA, *Time*, December 1, 1952

Natural Law

If you do something once, people will call it an accident. If you do it twice, they call it a coincidence. But do it a third time, you've just proven a natural law.
— GRACE MURRAY HOPPER, in *Mothers of Invention*, by E. A. Vare and G. Ptacek, 1987

Nature

The good news may be that Nature is phasing out the white man, but the bad news is that's who She thinks we all are.
— ALICE MALSENIOR WALKER, *Black Scholar*, spring 1982

Nature is commonplace. Imitation is more interesting.
— GERTRUDE STEIN, quoted in Sir Charles Spencer Chaplin, *My Autobiography*, 1964

New York

After nightfall, I wouldn't leave a burning building without an escort.
— HARRIET VAN HORNE, on muggings in Manhattan in the *Washington Post*, February 26, 1969

 *Novels*

This is not a novel to be tossed aside lightly. It should be thrown with great force.

— DOROTHY PARKER, book review, in *The Algonquin Wits,* Robert E. Drennan (ed), 1968

You should only read what is truly good or what is frankly bad.

— GERTRUDE STEIN, quoted in Ernest Hemingway, *A Moveable Feast,* 1964

 *Nursing*

No man (not even a doctor), ever gives any other definition of what a nurse should be than this—"devoted and obedient." This definition would do just as well for a porter. It might even do for a horse. It would not do for a policeman.

— FLORENCE NIGHTINGALE, *Notes on Nursing,* 1859

 *Obstacles*

In the face of an obstacle which is impossible to overcome, stubbornness is stupid.

— SIMONE DE BEAUVOIR, *The Ethics of Ambiguity,* 1948

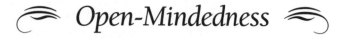

Open-Mindedness

Ah, snug lie those that slumber
Beneath Conviction's roof
Their floors are sturdy lumber;
Their windows weatherproof.
But I sleep cold forever
And cold sleep all my kind,
For I was born to shiver
In the draft from an open mind.

> ← PHYLLIS MCGINLEY, "Lament for a Wavering Viewpoint," *A Pocketful of Wry,* 1940

Opera

Going to the opera, like getting drunk, is a sin that carries its own punishment with it.

> ← HANNAH MORE, letter to her sister (1775), in *The Letters of Hannah More,* 1925

Pain

Pain gives us everything we need . . .
She gives us our strange souls and our peculiar thoughts,
She gives us all of life's highest winnings
Love, solitude and the face of death.

> ← EDITH SODERGRAN, "Pain" (1916), in Samuel Charters (trans), *We Women,* 1977

Palimony

If a man wants to leave a toothbrush at my house, he can damn
well marry me.

— MICHELLE TRIOLA MARVIN, on winning $104,000 California
Superior Court case against common-law husband Lee Marvin,
New York Times, April 19, 1979

(*See also* Divorce)

Parenting

The real menace in dealing with a 5 year old is that in no time at all
you begin to sound like a 5 year old.

— JEAN KERR, *Please Don't Eat the Daisies*, 1957

As long as any adult thinks that he, like the parents and teachers of
old, [can invoke] his own youth to understand the youth before
him, he is lost.

— MARGARET MEAD, *Culture and Commitment*, 1970

Most American children suffer too much mother and too little
father.

— GLORIA STEINEM, *New York Times*, August 26, 1971

Providing for one's family as a good husband and father is a water-
tight excuse for making money hand over fist. Greed may be a sin,
exploitation of other people might . . . look rather nasty, but who
can blame a man for "doing the best" for his children?

— EVA FIGES, *Nova*, 1973

(*See also* Adolescence, Childhood, Children, Daughters, Family,
Fathers, Grandparents, Mothers, Mothers and Sons, Mothers-
Daughters, Teenagers, Youth)

Parting

If I can let you go as trees let go
. . . Lose what I lose to keep what I can keep,
The strong root still alive under the snow,
Love will endure—if I can let you go.
— MAY SARTON, "The Autumn Sonnets," *A Durable Fire,* 1972

If you never want to see a man again, say "I love you, I want to marry you, I want to have children." They leave skid marks.
— RITA RUDNER, attributed, *The Penguin Book of Women's Humour,* Regina Barreca (ed), 1996

Leaving can sometimes be the best way to never go away.
— CATHY N. DAVIDSON, *36 Views of Mount Fuji,* 1993

All discarded lovers should be given a second chance, but with somebody else.
— MAE WEST, in Joseph Weintraub (ed), *The Wit and Wisdom of Mae West,* 1967

Ah, the relationships we get into just to get out of the ones we are not brave enough to say are over.
— JULIA PHILLIPS, *You'll Never Eat Lunch in This Town Again,* 1991

Somehow, the real moment of parting always precedes the physical act of separation.
— PRINCESS MARTHE BIBESCO, *Catherine-Paris,* 1928

(*See also* Absence, Alone, Betrayal, Breaking Up, Divorce, Estrangement, Farewell, Parting)

Passion

Wild Nights—Wild Nights
Were I with thee
Wild Nights should be
Our luxury!
> — EMILY DICKINSON, in T. W. Higginson and Mabel Loomis Todd
> (eds), *Poems by Emily Dickinson,* 1891

How little do they know human nature, who think they can say to
passion, so far shalt thou go, and no farther!
> — SARAH SCOTT, *The History of Cornelia,* 1750

Great passions, my dear, don't exist; they're liars' fantasies. What
do exist are little loves that may last for a short or a longer while.
> — ANNA MAGNANI, in Orianna Fallaci, *Limelighters,* 1963

There's plenty of fire in the coldest flint!
> — RACHEL FIELD, *All This and Heaven Too!* 1939

(*See also* Love, Sex, Sexuality)

Past

The past, with its pleasure, its rewards, its foolishness, its punish-
ments, is there for each of us forever, and it should be.
> — LILLIAN HELLMAN, *Scoundrel Time,* 1976

(*See also* Age, Memories)

Peace

You cannot shake hands with a clenched fist.
— INDIRA GANDHI, *Christian Science Monitor,* May 17, 1982

Perseverance

When people keep telling you that you can't do a thing, you kind of like to try it.
— MARGARET CHASE SMITH, **announcing her presidential candidacy, 1964**

Women must try to do things as men have tried. When they fail their failure must be but a challenge to others.
— AMELIA EARHART, in *The Sound of Wings,* by Mary S. Lovell, 1989

Personal Ads

What everyone's groping for, through the artificial mists, is harder to put into an ad; the touch of kindred, the shared current of light.
— BARBARA HOLLAND, *One's Company,* 1992

Philosophy

My definition of a philosopher is of a man up in a balloon, with his family and friends holding the ropes which confine him to earth and trying to haul him down.
— LOUISA MAY ALCOTT, in *Life, Letters and Journals,* E. D. Cheney (ed), 1889

Poetry

Our poems will have failed if our readers are not brought by them beyond the poems.
— MURIEL RUKEYSER, *The Life of Poetry,* 1949

Poetry is the natural language of all religions.
— MADAME DE STAËL, *De l'Allemagne,* 1810

The joy of poetry is that it will wait for you. Novels don't wait for you. Characters change. But poetry will wait. I think it's the greatest art.
— SONIA SANCHEZ, in *Voice of Freedom,* by Henry Hampton, 1990

Politicians

What troubles me is not that movie stars run for office, but that they find it easy to get elected. It should be difficult. It should be difficult for millionaires, too.
— SHANA ALEXANDER, *Life,* July 8, 1966

Politics

If you want to cut your own throat, don't come to me for a bandage.
— MARGARET THATCHER, comment to Robert Mugabe, Prime Minister of Zimbabwe, when he pressed for sanctions against South Africa, quoted in *Time,* July 7, 1986

The British Civil Service is a beautifully designed and effective braking mechanism.
— BARONESS WILLIAMS, Shirley Vivien Teresa Brittain, speech at the Royal Institute of Public Administration, February 11, 1980

I always cheer up immensely if an attack is particularly wounding because . . . it means that they have not a single political argument left.

— MARGARET THATCHER, in the *Daily Telegraph*, March 21, 1986

You can put lipstick on a hog and it's still a pig.

— ANN RICHARDS, on Republicans' attempts to improve their candidates, in *Sunday Morning* (CBS-TV), October 25, 1992

What this country needs is more unemployed politicians.

— ANGELA DAVIS, Speech, 1967

I don't think most people associate me with leeches or how to get them off. But I know how to get them off. I'm an expert at it.

— NANCY REAGAN, to the American Camping Association, March 2, 1987

I haven't the heart to take a minute from the men. The poor dears love it so.

— HATTIE WYATT CARAWAY, explaining why she never made a speech during 13 years as the first woman in the U.S. Senate, in *Washington Goes to War,* 1988

Politics is the process of getting along with the querulous, the garrulous and the congenitally unlovable.

— MARILYN MOATS KENNEDY, in "Playing Office Politics," *Newsweek,* September 16, 1985

(*See also* Activism, Autocrats, Politicians)

Pollution

As crude a weapon as the caveman's club, the chemical barrage has been hurled against the fabric of life.

— RACHEL CARSON, *Silent Spring,* 1962

 *Pornography*

We are unalterably opposed to the presentation of the female body being stripped, bound, raped, tortured, mutilated, and murdered in the name of commercial entertainment and free speech.
— SUSAN BROWNMILLER, *Against Our Will*, 1975

 *Poverty*

Among poor people, there's not any question about women being strong—even stronger than men—they work in the fields right along with the men. When your survival is at stake, you don't have these questions about yourself like middle-class women do.
— DOLORES HUERTA, in "Dolores Huerta: La Pasionaria of the Farmworkers," by Judith Coburn, in *Ms*, November 1976

Poverty isn't being broke; poverty is never having enough.
— BETTY JANE WYLIE, *Everywoman's Money Book*, 1989

Poverty is the great reality. That is why the artist seeks it.
— ANAÏS NIN, *Diary*, summer 1937

 *Praise*

Praise out of season, or tactlessly bestowed, can freeze the heart as much as blame.
— PEARL S. BUCK, *To My Daughters, With Love*, 1967

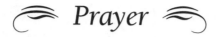 *Prayer*

Prayer is the language of the heart.
— Grace Aguilar, *The Spirit of Judaism*, 1842

To pray only when in peril is to use safety belts only in heavy traffic.
— Corrie ten Boom, *Don't Wrestle, Just Nestle*, 1978

Prayer is a long rope with a strong hold.
— Harriet Beecher Stowe, *The Pearl of Orr's Island*, 1862

Did not God
Sometimes withhold in mercy what we ask
We should be ruin'd at our own request
— Hannah Moore, *Sacred Dogmas*, 1782

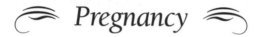 *Pregnancy*

The trouble with getting introspective when you're pregnant is that you never know who you might run into.
— Carrie Fisher, *Delusions of Grandma*, 1994

I was slowly taking on the dimensions of a chest of drawers.
— Maria Augusta Trapp, *The Story of the Trapp Family Singers*, 1949

Her child was like a load that held her down and yet like a hand that pulled her to her feet.
— Edith Wharton, **Summer**, 1918

If pregnancy were a book, they would cut the last two chapters.
— Nora Ephron, **Heartburn**, 1983

Prejudice

Prejudices, it is well known, are most difficult to eradicate from the heart whose soil has never been loosened or fertilized by education; they grow there, firm as weeds among stones.
— EMILY BRONTË, *Jane Eyre,* 1847

It's like a hair across your cheek. You can't see it, you can't find it with your fingers, but you keep brushing at it because the feel of it is irritating.
— MARIAN ANDERSON, with Emily Kimbrough, in *Ladies Home Journal,* 1960

Prejudice, like fear, is acquired.
— MARIE KILLILEA, *Karen,* 1952

Prejudice squints when it looks and lies when it talks.
— LAURE JUNOT, Duchesse de Abrantes, *Memoirs of Madame Junot,* 1883

Pride

Never bend your head. Always hold it high. Look the world straight in the eye.
— HELEN KELLER, advice to a 5-year-old, recalled on her death, June 1, 1968

Privacy

There are many things in your heart you can never tell to another person. They are you, your private joys and sorrows, and you can never tell them. You cheapen yourself, the inside of yourself, when you tell them.

↞ GRETA GARBO, in *The Story of Great Garbo,* by Bruce Biery, 1928

Privacy is a privilege not granted to the aged or the young.

↞ MARGRET LAURENCE, *The Stone Angel,* 1964

Problems

It's odd that you can get so anesthetized by your own pain or your own problem that you don't quite fully share the hell of someone close to you.

↞ LADY BIRD JOHNSON, *A White House Diary,* 1970

When one's own problems are unsolvable and all best efforts frustrated, it is lifesaving to listen to other people's problems.

↞ SUZANNE MASSIE, *Journey,* 1975

She did observe, with some dismay, that far from conquering all, love lazily sidestepped practical problems.

↞ JEAN STAFFORD, "The Liberation," *The Collected Stories of Jean Stafford,* 1969

Make sure you never, never argue at night. You just lose a good night's sleep and you can't settle anything until morning anyway.

↞ ROSE KENNEDY, **advice to her first married granddaughter,** *People,* January 6, 1983

She probably labored under the common delusion that you made things better by talking about them.

　　— ROSE MACAULEY, *Crewe Train*, 1926

(*See also* Adversity)

Promiscuity

I consider promiscuity immoral. Not because sex is evil, but because sex is too good and too important.

　　— AYN RAND, *Playboy,* March 1964

(*See also* Sex)

Psychotherapy

Life itself remains a very effective therapist.

　　— DR. KAREN HORNEY, recalled on her death, December 4, 1952

Questions

Once you start asking questions, innocence is gone.

　　— MARY ASTOR, *A Life on Film,* 1967

There are no right answers to wrong questions.

　　— URSULA LE GUIN, *Planet of Exile,* 1975

Children ask better questions than do adults. "May I have a cookie?" "Why is the sky blue?" and "What does a cow say?" are far more likely to elicit a cheerful response than "Where's your manuscript?" "What haven't you called?" and "Who's your lawyer?"

　　— FRAN LEBOWITZ, *Metropolitan Life,* 1974

 *Quitting*

The more you kick something that's dead the worse it smells.
— BARBARA STANWYCK, in Al DiOrio, *Barbara Stanwyck,* 1984

There comes a time when every scientist, even God, has to write off an experiment.
— P. D. JAMES, *Devices and Desires,* 1989

 *Quotations*

An apt quotation is like a lamp which flings its light over the whole sentence.
— I. E. LANDON, *Romance and Reality,* 1831

I always have a quotation for everything—it saves original thinking.
— DOROTHY L. SAYERS, 1932

The everlasting quotation-lover dotes on the husks of learning.
— MARIA EDGEWORTH, *Thoughts on Bores,* 1826

I love [quotations] because it is a joy to find thoughts one might have, beautifully expressed with much authority by someone recognizedly wiser than oneself.
— MARLENE DIETRICH, *Marlene Dietrich's ABC,* 1986

 *Racism*

Sister! Your foot's smaller but it's still on my neck.
— PAT PARKER, *Movement in Black,* 1978

Racism is so universal in this country, so widespread and deepseated, that it is invisible because it is so normal.

— SHIRLEY CHISHOLM, *Unbought and Unbossed,* 1970

In the last few years, race relations in America have entered upon a period of intensified craziness wherein fear of being called a racist has so thoroughly overwhelmed fear of being a racist that we are in danger of losing sight of the distinction.

— FLORENCE KING, *Lump It or Leave It,* 1990

 *Rape*

Rape is a culturally fostered means of suppressing women. Legally we say we deplore it, but mythically we romanticize and perpetuate it, and privately we excuse and overlook it.

— VICTORIA BILLINGS, *The Womansbook,* 1974

Rape is nothing more or less than a conscious process of intimidation by which all men keep all women in a state of fear.

— SUSAN BROWNMILLER, *Against Our Will,* 1975

Perhaps it is the only crime in which the victim becomes the accused.

— FREDA ADLER, *Sisters in Crime,* 1975

Bad judgment and carelessness are not punishable by rape.

— PEARL CLEAGE, *Deals with the Devil,* 1993

 *Reading*

Children are made readers on the laps of their parents.

— EMILIE BUCHWALD, speech, 1994

She read Dickens in the spirit in which she would have eloped with him.

— EUDORA WELTY, *One Writer's Beginnings,* 1984

Until I feared I would lose it, I never loved to read. One does not love breathing.

— HARPER LEE, *To Kill a Mockingbird,* 1960

If at the end of the saddest the most disappointing and hurtful day, each one of us may come to a quiet room somewhere, and that room his own, if there is a light burning above white pillows and a pile of books waiting under the light, then indeed we may still praise Allah, that He has not terminated all the Delights.

— KATHLEEN NORRIS, *These I Like Best,* 1941

(*See also* Books, Literature, Novels, Stories, Words)

Reality

Reality is a crutch for people who can't cope with drugs.

— JANE WAGNER, *Appearing Nitely,* 1977

Fearful as reality is, it is less fearful than evasions of reality. . . . Look steadfastly into the slit, pin-pointed malignant eyes of reality as an old-hand trainer dominates his wild beasts.

— CAITLIN THOMAS, *Not Quite Posthumous Letter to My Daughter,* 1963

What is reality anyway? Nothin' but a collective hunch.

— JANE WAGNER, *The Search for Intelligent Life in the Universe,* 1985

Regret

Never regret. If it's good, it's wonderful. If it's bad, it's experience.
　　— VICTORIA HOLT, *The Black Opal*, 1993

The bitterest tears shed over graves are for words left unsaid and deeds left undone.
　　— HARRIET BEECHER STOWE, *Little Foxes*, 1865

If eternal life can be given
let me have it again as a child
among those whom I did not love
enough, while they lived
　　— GWEN HARWOOD, *Bone Scan*, 1988

Regrets are as personal as fingerprints.
　　— MARGARET CULKIN BANNING, "Living With Regrets," *Reader's Digest*, October 1958

Relationships

Now the whole dizzying and delirious range of sexual possibilities has been boiled down to that one big, boring, bulimic word: Relationship.
　　— JULIE BURCHILL, "The Dead Zone," in *Arena*, 1988

If one is out of touch with oneself, then one cannot touch others.
　　— ANNE MORROW LINDBERGH, *Gifts from the Sea*, 1955

We had a lot in common. I loved him and he loved him.
　　— SHELLEY WINTERS, in Susan Strasberg, *Bittersweet*, 1980

A relationship isn't meant to be an insurance policy, a life preserver or a security blanket.
— DIANE CROWLEY, column, 1992

We can only love a person who eats what we eat.
— RIGOBERTA MENCHU, in Elisabeth Burgos-Debray (ed), *I, Rigoberta Menchu*, 1983

Kindness and intelligence don't always deliver us from the pitfalls and traps: there are always failures of love, of will, of imagination. There is no way to take the danger out of human relationships.
— BARBARA GRIZZUTI HARRISON, "Secrets Women Tell Each Other," in *McCall's*, August 1975

Do you want me to tell you something really subversive? Love is everything it's cracked up to be.
— ERICA JONG, *How to Save Your Own Life*, 1977

We want to be part of a couple. Uncoupled, we are all slightly diminished in sheer bulk. . . . there's a danger in certain moods and at certain times of year, of simply blowing off the face of the world like a scrap of crumbled paper.
— BARBARA HOLLAND, *One's Company*, 1992

(*See also* Children, Dating, Marriage, Parenting)

Religion

Parsons always seem to be specially horrified about things like sunbathing and naked bodies. They don't mind poverty and misery and cruelty to animals nearly so much.
— SUSAN ERTZ, *The Story of Julian*, 1931

Religion does not confirm that there are hungry people in the world; it interprets the hungry to be our brethren whom we allow to starve.

— DOROTHEE SOLLE, *Death by Bread Alone,* 1975

A moment of silence is not inherently religious.

— SANDRA DAY O'CONNOR, **Supreme Court ruling, June 4, 1985**

You've got to have something to eat and a little love in your life before you can hold still for any damn body's sermon on how to behave.

— BILLIE HOLIDAY, **with William Duffy,** *Lady Sings the Blues,* 1956

It would be easier to peel off a three-day-old Band-Aid from a hairy kneecap than to remove the patina of Baptist upbringing that coats my psyche.

— MARY ELLEN SNODGRASS, *Growing Up Baptist,* 1989

There is no religion without love, and people may talk as much as they like about their religion, but if it does not teach them to be good and kind to man and beast, it is all a sham.

— ANNA SEWELL, *Black Beauty,* 1877

Religion is love; in no case is it logic.

— BEATRICE POTTER WEBB, *My Apprenticeship,* 1926

It is difficult to discern a serious threat to religious liberty from a room of silent, thoughtful schoolchildren.

— SANDRA DAY O'CONNOR, **Supreme Court ruling, June 4, 1985**

(*See also* Christianity, Church, God, Prayer, Spirituality)

Responsibility

People tend to forget their duties but remember their rights.
— INDIRA GANDHI, *Last Words*, 1984

Responsibility is the price every man must pay for freedom.
— EDITH HAMILTON, in Doris Fielding Reid, *Edith Hamilton*, 1967

Parents can only give good advice or put them on the right paths, but the final forming of a person's character lies in their own hands.
— ANNE FRANK, *The Diary of a Young girl*, 1952

Retirement

Retirement may be looked upon either as a prolonged holiday or as a rejection, a being thrown on to the scrap heap.
— SIMONE DE BEAUVOIR, *The Coming of Age*, 1970

I married him for better or worse, but not for lunch.
— HAZEL WEISS, on husband George Weiss's retirement as general manager of the New York Yankees, in Lee Green, *Sportswit*, 1984

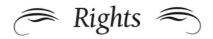

Rights

Where after all, do human rights begin? They begin in small places, close to home—so close and so small that they cannot be seen on any map of the world.
— ELEANOR ROOSEVELT, in *The New York Times*, December 26, 1965

My greatest disappointment in all the projects I worked on during the White House years was the failure of the Equal Rights Amendment to be ratified. Why all the controversy and why such difficulty in giving women the protection of the Constitution that should have been theirs long ago?
— ROSALYNN CARTER, *First Lady From Plains,* 1984

A right which goes unrecognized by anybody is not worth very much.
— SIMONE WEIL, *The Need for Roots,* 1949

There is but one honest limit to the rights of a sentient being; it is where they touch the rights of another sentient being.
— FRANCES WRIGHT, *Course of Popular Lectures,* 1829

I recognize no rights but human rights—I know nothing of men's rights and women's rights.
— ANGELINA E. GRIMKÉ (1837), *Letters to Catherine E. Beecher,* 1969

Risk

A ship in port is safe, but that's not what ships are built for.
— GRACE MURRAY HOPPER, U.S. mathematician, computer scientist, naval admiral, "The Judge," in Roger von Oech, *A Kick in the Seat of the Pants,* 1986

If you're not living on the edge, you're taking up too much room.
— LORRAINE TEEL, in *Minnesota Women's Press* (1996)

Just because you don't act everywhere doesn't mean you can't act anywhere.
— MADELEINE ALBRIGHT, U.S. Secretary of State, *Time* magazine interview, 1999

It is often easier to apologize than to get permission.
— GRACE MURRAY HOPPER, Grace Murray Hopper (interview)

We haven't been properly programmed for taking chances. If we strike oil in the flower bed, we look around for some man to sell the rights to for $50, because what do we know about oil?

— BARBARA HOLLAND, *One's Company*, 1992

It seems that it is madder never to abandon one's self than often to be infatuated; better to be wounded, a captive and a slave, than always to walk in armor.

— MARGARET FULLER, *Summer on the Lakes*, 1844

(*See also* Adventure)

Romance

In real love you want the other person's good. In romantic love, you want the other person.

— MARGARET ANDERSON, *The Fiery Fountains*, 1953

I used to think romantic love was a neurosis shared by two, a supreme foolishness. I no longer thought that. There's nothing foolish in loving anyone. Thinking you'll be loved in return is what's foolish.

— RITA MAE BROWN, *Bingo*, 1988

Romantic love has always seemed to me unaccountable, unassailable, unforgettable, and nearly always unattainable.

— MARGARET ANDERSON, *The Fiery Fountains*, 1953

(*See also* Affairs, Dating, First Love, Free Love, Heart, Love, Love Letters, Loving, Mature Love, May-December Romance, Memories of Love, Sex, Sexuality, True Love)

Roots

I am a turtle. Wherever I go I carry "home" on my back.
 ⟶ GLORIA ANZALDUA, *Borderland/La Frontera*, 1987

That I can live long enough
To obtain one and only one desire—
That someday I can see again
The mulberry and catalpa trees of home.
 ⟶ TS'AI YEN, "Eighteen Verses Sung to a Tatar Reed Whistle"
 (c. 200), in Joanna Bankier and Deirdre Lashgari (eds), *Women
 Poets of the World*, 1983

Royalty

We'll go quietly.
 ⟶ QUEEN ELIZABETH II, at the suggestion that Great Britain might
 someday want a republic, in Ann Morrow, *The Queen*, 1983

To be a King and to wear a crown is a thing more glorious to them
that see it than it is pleasant to them that bear it.
 ⟶ QUEEN ELIZABETH I, address to parliament, 1601

There are few prisoners more closely guarded than princes.
 ⟶ CHRISTINA, Queen of Sweden, in Henry Woodhead, *Memoirs of
 Christina, Queen of Sweden*, 1862

I am said to be the most beautiful woman in Europe. About that, of
course, I cannot judge because I cannot know. But about the other
queens, I know. I am the most beautiful queen in Europe.
 ⟶ QUEEN MARIE OF RUMANIA (1919), in Hannah Pakula, *The Last
 Romantic*, 1984

My seat has been the seat of kings, and I will have no rascal to succeed me.

   — ELIZABETH I (1603), on her deathbed when pressed about a successor, in Mrs. Jameson, *Memoirs of Celebrated Female Sovereigns,* 1831

 **Rudeness**

Ideological differences are no excuse for rudeness.

   — JUDITH MARTIN, *Miss Manners' Guide to Excruciatingly Correct Behavior,* 1982

You can't be truly rude until you understand good manners.

   — RITA MAE BROWN, *Starting From Scratch,* 1988

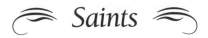 **Rumor**

It is harder to kill a whisper than even a shouted calumny.

   — MARY STEWART, *The Last Enchantment,* 1979

There is a vital force in rumor. Though crushed to earth, to all intents and purposes buried, it can rise again without apparent effort.

   — ELEANOR ROBSON BELMONT, *The Fabric of Memory,* 1957

 **Saints**

Don't call me a saint. I don't want to be dismissed that easily.

   — DOROTHY DAY, in Robert Ellsberg (ed), *By Little and By Little,* 1983

A saint is simply a human being whose soul has grown up to its full stature.

   — EVELYN UNDERHILL, *Concerning the Inner Life,* 1926

The wonderful thing about saints is that they were human. They lost their tempers, got hungry, scolded God, were egotistical or testy or impatient in their turns, made mistakes and regretted them. Still they went on doggedly blundering toward heaven.
— PHYLLIS MCGINLEY, *Saint-Watching,* 1969

Scandal

The scandal is often worse than the sin itself.
— MARGUERITE D'ANGOULÊME, *Heptameron,* 1558

Sea

In the biting honesty of salt, the sea makes her secrets known to those who care to listen.
— SANDRA BENITEZ, *A Place Where the Sea Remembers,* 1993

The mysterious human bond with the great seas that poets write about has a physiological base in our veins and in every living thing, where runs fluid of the same saline proportions as ocean water.
— ANNE W. SIMON, *The Thin Edge,* 1978

The voice of the sea speaks to the soul.
— KATE CHOPIN, *The Awakening,* 1899

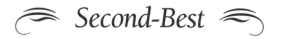

Second-Best

There is only one real sin, and that is to persuade oneself that second-best is anything but the second best.
— DORIS MAY LESSING, *The Golden Notebook,* 1962

Secrets

I will have no locked cupboards in my life.
— GERTRUDE BELL, in Janet Courtney, *An Oxford Portrait Gallery,*
1931

Sometimes you just gotta trust that your secret's been kept long
enough.
— ANNE CAMERON, *Daughters of Copper Woman,* 1981

A person who has no secrets is a liar.
— ANNE ROIPHE, *Lovingkindness,* 1987

Self-Esteem

We cease loving ourselves when no one loves us.
— MADAME DE STAËL, in *Portraits of Women,* 1891

You can be pleased with nothing when you are not pleased with
yourself.
— LADY MARY WORTLEY MONTAGU (1712), in Octave Thanet (ed),
The Best Letters of Lady Mary Wortley Montagu, 1901

She's been so programmed by Julian to think of herself as inferior
material that if a man threw himself at her feet, her immediate reac-
tion would be to call an ambulance.
— LUCILLE KALLEN, *Introducing C. B. Greenfield,* 1979

To say something nice about themselves, this is the hardest thing in
the world for people to do. They'd rather take their clothes off.
— NANCY FRIDAY, *My Mother/My Self,* 1977

Self-Importance

She invents dramas in which she always stars.
— ANAÏS NIN, *The Diary of Anaïs Nin*, 1966

Nine tenths of our suffering is caused by others not thinking so much of us as we think they ought.
— MARY LYON, in Van Wyck Brooks (ed), *The Journal of Gamaliel Bradford*, 1953

He thinks he's finer than frog hair.
— JESSAMYN WEST, *The Massacre at Fall Creek*, 1975

Sex

The day after that wedding night I found that a distance of a thousand miles, abyss and discovery and irremediable metamorphosis, separated me from the day before.
— COLETTE, *Noces*, 1945

Aren't women prudes if they don't and prostitutes if they do?
— KATE MILLETT, speech at the Women Writer's Conference in Los Angeles, March 22, 1975

A man wants what a woman has—sex. He can steal it (rape), persuade her to give it away (seduction), rent it (prostitution), lease it over the long term (marriage in the United States) or own it outright (marriage in most societies).
— ANDREA DWORKIN, in *Ms*, December 1976

It is better to be first with an ugly woman than the hundredth with a beauty.
— PEARL S. BUCK, *The Good Earth*, 1931

It doesn't matter what you do in the bedroom as long as you don't do it in the street and frighten the horses.

— MRS. PATRICK CAMPBELL, in Daphne Fielding, *The Duchess of Jermyn Street*

In my day, I would only have sex with a man if I found him extremely attractive. These days, girls seem to choose them in much the same way as they might choose to suck on a boiled sweet.

— MARY WESLEY, *Independent,* October 18, 1997

When you look back on your life and try to figure out where you've been and where you are going, when you look at your work, your love affairs, your marriages, your children, your pain, your happiness—when you examine all that closely, what you really find out is that the only person you really want to go to bed with is yourself.

— SHIRLEY MacLAINE, *Washington Post,* November 14, 1977

Nobody dies from lack of sex. It's lack of love we die from.

— MARGARET ATWOOD, *The Handmaid's Tale,* 1985

Women complain about sex more often than men. Their gripes fall into two major categories: (1) Not enough. (2) Too much.

— ANN LANDERS, *Truth Is Stranger,* 1968

Heaven and earth! How is it that bodies join but never meet?

— BEAH RICHARDS, "It's Time for Love," in *A Black Woman Speaks and Other Poems,* 1974

Plenty of guys are good at sex, but conversation, now there's an art.

— LINDA BARNES, A Trouble of Fools, 1987

(*See also* Affairs, Birth Control, Dating, First Love, Free Love, Heart, Love, Loving, Mature Love, May-December Romance, Sex Object, Sexuality)

 *Sex Education*

Most mothers think that to keep young people away from love-making, it is enough never to mention it in front of them.
— MARIE MADELEINE DE LA FAYETTE, *The Princess of Clèves*, 1678

Before the child ever gets to school it will have received crucial, almost irrevocable sex education and this will have been taught by the parents, who are not aware of what they are doing.
— MARY CALDERONE, in *People*, 1980

 *Sex Objects*

It takes two to make a woman into a sex object.
— ELAINE MORGAN, *The Descent of Woman*, 1972

If people are worried about unfair advancement, they should look at the sons-in-law of the world running companies. They've truly slept their way to the top.
— MARY CUNNINGHAM, in Bob Chieger, *Was It Good for You, Too?* 1983

A sex symbol becomes a thing. I hate being a thing.
— MARILYN MONROE in *Uncommon Scold*, by Abby Adams, 1989

(*See also* Affairs, Dating, Sex, Sexuality)

 *Sexuality*

When she raises her eyelids, it's as if she were taking off her clothes.
— COLETTE, *Claudine and Annie*, 1903

A full bosom is actually a millstone around a woman's neck.
— GERMAINE GREER, *The Female Eunuch*, 1970

He was the kind of guy who could kiss you behind your ear and make you feel like you'd just had kinky sex.
— JULIA ALVAREZ, *How the Garcia Girls Lost Their Accents*, 1991

Sex appeal is 50% what you've got and 50% what people think you've got.
— SOPHIA LOREN, in *Halliwell's Filmgoer's Companion*, by Leslie Halliwell, 1984

The average man is more interested in a woman who is interested in him than he is in a woman—any woman—with beautiful legs.
— MARLENE DIETRICH, attributed, 1954

(*See also* Affairs, Dating, Sex)

Shadows

Never fear shadows. They simply mean there's a light shining somewhere nearby.
— RUTH RENKEL, in *Reader's Digest*, 1983

It's harder to shake off shadows than realities sometimes.
— RACHEL FIELD, *And Now Tomorrow*, 1942

Siblings

We were like ill-assorted animals tied to a common tethering post.
— JESSICA MITFORD, *Daughters and Rebels*, 1960

We know one another's faults, virtues, catastrophes, mortifications, triumphs, rivalries, desires, and how long we can each hang by our hands to a bar. We have been banded together under pack codes and tribal laws.

— ROSE MACAULEY, *Personal Pleasures,* 1936

 *Silence*

Every day silence harvests its victims. Silence is a mortal illness.

— NATALIA GINZBURG, *The Little Virtues,* 1962

Learn to get in touch with silence within yourself and know that everything in life has a purpose.

— ELISABETH KÜBLER-ROSS, In *Yoga Journal,* November 1, 1976

 *Simplicity*

I long for a Japanese sort of existence. Each member of the family with a grass mat to sleep on, a change of clothes, a bowl, a cup, a pair of chopsticks. Nothing else. Think how clean it would be.

— BARBARA HOLLAND, *In Private Life,* 1997

We can do no great things—only small things with great love.

— MOTHER TERESA, in Kathryn Spink (ed), *In the Silence of the Heart,* 1983

One of the secrets of a happy life is continuous small treats.

— IRIS MURDOCH, *The Sea, the Sea,* 1978

Neglecting small things because one wishes to do great things is the excuse of the faint-hearted.

— ALEXANDRA DAVID-NEEL, *La Lampe de Sagesse,* 1986

Sin

All sins are attempts to fill voids.

— SIMONE WEIL, *La Pesanteur et la Grâce,* 1946

Many are saved from sin by being so inept at it.

— MIGNON MCLAUGHLIN, *The Neurotic's Notebook,* 1963

People are no longer sinful, they are only immature or underprivileged or frightened, or more particularly, sick.

— PHYLLIS MCGINLEY, *The Province of the Heart,* 1959

Sisters

Your sister is the only creature on earth who shares your heritage, history, environment, DNA, bone structure, and contempt for stupid Aunt Gertie.

— LINDA SUNSHINE, *Mom Loves Me Best,* 1990

If you don't understand how a woman could both love her sister dearly and want to wring her neck at the same time, then you were probably an only child.

— LINDA SUNSHINE, *Mom Loves Me Best,* 1990

Both within the family and without, our sisters hold up our mirrors: our images of who we are and of who we can dare to become.

— ELIZABETH FIELD, *Sisters,* 1979

A sister is both your mirror and your opposite.

— ELIZABETH FISHEL, *People,* June 2, 1980

Of two sisters
one is always the watcher
one the dancer
—— LOUISE GLUCK, *Descending Figure,* 1980

More than Santa Claus, your sister knows when you've been bad and good.
—— LINDA SUNSHINE, *Mom Loves Me Best,* 1990

Between sisters, often, the child's cry never dies down. "Never leave me," it says, "do not abandon me."
—— LOUISE BERNIKOW, *Among Women,* 1980

Sisters are probably the most competitive relationship within the family, but once the sisters are grown, it becomes the strongest relationship.
—— MARGARET MEAD, in Elizabeth Fishel, *Sisters,* 1979

It is natural not to care about a sister, certainly not when she is four years older and grinds her teeth at night.
—— GERTRUDE STEIN, *Everybody's Autobiography,* 1937

My sister and I may have been crafted of the same genetic clay, baked in the same uterine kiln, but we were disparate species, doomed never to love each other except blindly.
—— JUDITH KELMAN, *Where Shadows Fall,* 1987

A baby sister is nicer than a goat. You'll get used to her.
—— LYNNE ALPERN and ESTHER BLUMENFELD, *Oh, Lord, I Sound Just Like Mamma,* 1986

What surprised me was that within a family, the voices of sisters as they're talking are virtually always the same.
—— ELIZABETH FISHER, *Sisters,* 1979

Sleep

To sleep is an act of faith.
　―Barbara Grizzuti Harrison, *Foreign Bodies*, 1984

Sleep is death without the responsibility.
　―Fran Lebowitz, *Metropolitan Life*, 1978

Blessed be sleep! We are all young then; we are all happy. Then our dead are living.
　―Fanny Fern, *Ginger Snaps*, 1870

Most people spend their lives going to bed when they're not sleepy and getting up when they are.
　―Cindy Adams, in Joey Adams, *Cindy and I*, 1957

Smile

That grin! She could have taken it off her face and put it on the table.
　―Jean Stafford, *Bad Characters*, 1954

Social Change

Thinking about profound social change, conservatives always expect disaster, while revolutionaries confidently anticipate utopia. Both are wrong.
　―Carolyn Heilbrun, *Toward a Recognition of Androgyny*, 1973

Nearly all great civilizations that perished did so because they had crystallized, because they were incapable of adapting themselves to new conditions, new methods, new points of view. It is as though people would rather die than change.

　　— ELEANOR ROOSEVELT, *Tomorrow Is Now,* 1963

Whenever you take a step forward you are bound to disturb something. . . . When a whole society moves forward, this tramping is on a much bigger scale and each thing that you disturb, each vested interest which you want to remove, stands as an obstacle.

　　— INDIRA GANDHI, 1967, *Speeches and Writings,* 1975

 *Solitude*

There are days when solitude, for someone my age, is a heady wine that intoxicates you with freedom, others when it is a bitter tonic, and still others when it is a poison that makes you beat your head against the wall.

　　— COLETTE, *Les Villes de la Vigne,* 1908

Solitude is improved by being voluntary.

　　— BARBARA HOLLAND, *One's Company,* 1992

 *Sorrow*

It was the last night before sorrow touched her life; and no life is ever quite the same again when once that cold, sanctifying touch has been laid upon it.

　　— L. M. MONTGOMERY, *Anne of Green Gables,* 1908

Every sorrow suggests a thousand songs, and every song recalls a thousand sorrows.

　　— MARILYNNE ROBINSON, *Housekeeping,* 1980

Many people misjudge the permanent effect of sorrow, and their capacity to live in the past.
➤ IVY COMPTON-BURNETT, *Mother and Son*, 1955

The South

She had once been a Southern belle and she had never got over it.
➤ PEARL S. BUCK, *Fighting Angel*, 1936

In Georgia, no lady was supposed to know that she was a virgin until she ceased to be one.
➤ FRANCES NEWMAN, *The Hard-Boiled Virgin*, 1936

Southerners can never resist a losing cause.
➤ MARGARET MITCHELL, *Gone With the Wind*, 1936

To grow up female in the south is to inherit a set of directives that warp one for life, if they do not actually induce psychosis.
➤ SHIRLEY ABBOTT, *Womenfolks Growing Up Down South*, 1983

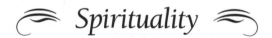

Spirituality

Spirituality leaps where science cannot yet follow, because science must always test and measure, and much of reality and human experience is immeasurable.
➤ STARHAWK, *The Spiral Dance*, 1979

O My Lord, if I worship Thee from fear of Hell, burn me in Hell, and if I worship Thee from hope of Paradise, exclude me thence, but if I worship Thee for Thine own sake then withhold not from me Thine Eternal Beauty.
➤ RABI'A THE MYSTIC (8th century), in Margaret Smith, *Rabi'a the Mystic*, 1928

There are two ways of spreading light: To be the candle or the mirror that reflects it.

    ➤ EDITH WHARTON, *Artemis to Actaeon and Other Verse,* 1909

The power to love what is purely abstract is given to few.

    ➤ MARGOT ASQUITH, *More or Less About Myself,* 1934

Sports

It's time to raise a generation of participants, not another generation of fans.

    ➤ JANICE KAPLAN, *Women and Sports,* 1979

Sport strips away personality, letting the white bone of character shine through.

    ➤ RITA MAE BROWN, *Sudden Death,* 1983

The real adherent of the sporting ethic knows that when she's wet, cold, hungry, sore, exhausted, and perhaps a little frightened, he's having a marvelous time.

    ➤ MRS. FALK FEELEY, *A Swarm of Wasps,* 1983

Spring

Forget not bees in winter, though they sleep, for winter's big with summer in her womb.

    ➤ VITA SACKVILLE-WEST, *The Land,* 1926

Suddenly a mist of green on the trees, as quiet as thought.

    ➤ DOROTHY RICHARDSON, *Pilgrimage: The Trap,* 1925

You've got maybe four special springs in your life; all the rest recall them.

    ➤ DIANE VREULS, *Are We There Yet,* 1975

Spring glides gradually into the farmer's consciousness, but on us city people it bursts with all the relish of a sudden surprise.

— Mrs. William Starr Dana, *According to Season,* 1894

Stars

It is strange that there are times when I feel the stars are not at all solemn; they are secretly gay.

— Katherine Mansfield (1920), *Journal of Katherine Mansfield,* 1927

Stock Market

Half of them don't know what's going to happen tomorrow, and the other half don't know that they don't know.

— Jane Bryant Quinn, **of stock market players, on CNN-TV, April 4, 1994**

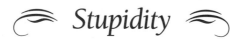

Stories

The universe is made of stories, not of atoms.

— Muriel Rukeyser, *The Speed of Darkness,* 1968

Stupidity

I'm patient with stupidity, but not with those who are proud of it.

— Edith Sitwell, in *Reader's Digest,* February 1, 1993

The difference between genius and stupidity is that even genius has its limits.

— Rita Mae Brown, *Bingo,* 1988

Style

Fashion can be bought. Style one must possess.
━ EDNA WOOLMAN CHASE, *Always in Vogue*, 1954

Success

Success can make you go one of two ways. It can make you a prima donna—or it can smooth the edges, take away the insecurities and let the nice things come out.
━ BARBARA WALTERS, in *Newsweek*, May 6, 1974

Success is a great deodorant.
━ ELIZABETH TAYLOR, ABC-TV, April 6, 1977

It is nothing to succeed if one has not taken great trouble, and it is nothing to fail if one has done the best one could.
━ NADIA BOULANGER, in Don Campbell, *Reflections of Boulanger,* 1982

Success is as ice cold and as lonely as the north pole.
━ VICKI BAUM, *Grand Hotel*, 1929

Success is counted sweetest
By those who ne'er succeed.
━ EMILY DICKINSON (1859), in *Poems by Emily Dickinson*, 1890

Looking at the glossy success of those women in magazines, most of us don't think "If she can do it, so can I." We think of her as an alien. . . . Certainly a bitch. Not nice like us.
━ BARBARA HOLLAND, *One's Company*, 1992

The person who knows "how" will always have a job. The person who knows "why" will always be his boss.
  ➤ DIANE SILVERS RAVITCH, **commencement address at Reed College, Portland, Oregon,** *Time,* **June 17, 1985**

If you think you can, you can. And if you think you can't, you're right.
  ➤ MARY KAY ASH, *New York Times,* October 20, 1985

I do not know anyone who has got to the top without hard work. That is the recipe. It will not always get you to the top, but should get you pretty near.
  ➤ MARGARET THATCHER, **London** *Daily Telegraph,* **March 21 1986**

I long to accomplish a great and noble task, but it is my chief duty to accomplish small tasks as if they were great and noble.
  ➤ HELEN KELLER, **recalled on her death, June 1, 1968**

I was brought up to believe that the only thing worth doing was to add to the sum of accurate information in the world.
  ➤ MARGARET MEAD, *New York Times,* August 9, 1964

 *Suffering*

Suffering is one of the ways of knowing you're alive.
  ➤ JESSAMYN WEST, *To See the Dream,* 1957

I do not believe that sheer suffering teaches. If suffering alone taught, all the world would be wise.
  ➤ ANNE MORROW LINDBERGH, *Hour of Gold, Hour of Lead,* 1973

Suffering raises up those souls that are truly great; it is only small souls that are made mean-spirited by it.
  ➤ ALEXANDRA DAVID-NEEL (1889), IN *LA LAMPE DE SAGESSE,* 1986

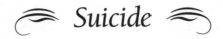

Suicide

If I cannot give consent to my own death, then whose body is this?
Who owns my life?
— SUE RODRIGUEZ, *Globe and Mail,* December 5, 1992

Summer

Summertime is the time of sharpest memory.
— RUTH SIDRANSKY, *In Silence,* 1990

Sunrise

Dawn is the child
wet with birth.
— CHARLOTTE DECLUE, in Joseph Bruchac (ed), *Songs From This Earth on Turtle's Back,* 1983

Most people do not consider dawn to be an attractive experience—
unless they are still up.
— ELLEN GOODMAN, *Close to Home,* 1979

Dawn and its excesses always reminded me of heaven, a place
where I have always known I would not be comfortable.
— MARILYNNE ROBINSON, *Housekeeping,* 1980

Sunset

The sun cast no rays, scarcely colored the sky around it, simply
hung there on the earth's rim like the burning heart of creation.
— MARTHA OSTENSO, *The Dark Dawn,* 1926

The sky broke like an egg into full sunset and the water caught fire.
— PAMELA HANSFORD JOHNSON, *The Unspeakable Skipton*, 1981

The pale, cold light of the winter sunset did not beautify—it was like the light of truth itself.
— WILLA CATHER, *My Ántonia*, 1918

Support

To keep a lamp burning we have to keep putting oil in it.
— MOTHER TERESA, in *Time*, December 29, 1975

There is no support so strong as the strength that enables one to stand alone.
— ELLEN GLASGOW, in *The Shadowy Third*, 1923

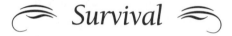

Survival

Misfortune had made Lily supple instead of hardening her, and a pliable substance is less easy to break than a stiff one.
— EDITH WHARTON, *The House of Mirth*, 1905

I have not withdrawn into despair, I did not go mad in gathering honey I did not go mad, I did not go mad, I did not go mad.
— HODA AL-NAMANI, in Elizabeth Warnock Fernea, *Women and the Family in the Middle East*, 1985

Tact

Tact is after all a kind of mind reading.
— SARAH ORNE JEWETT, *The Country of the Pointed Firs and Other Stories*, 1896

 *Talent*

Everyone has talent. What is rare is the courage to follow the talent to the dark place where it leads.
— ERICA JONG, in *Ms*, 1972

It is one thing to be gifted and quite another thing to be worthy of one's own gift.
— NADIA BOULANGER, *Reflections of Boulanger*, 1982

Great talent or small, it makes no difference . . . we never know if our technique has been adequate to the vision.
— MADELEINE L'ENGLE, *Two-Part Invention*, 1988

Talent is like electricity. . . . You can plug into it and light up a lamp, keep a heart pump going, light a cathedral, or you can electrocute a person with it. Electricity will do all that. It makes no judgement. I think talent is like that. I believe every person is born with talent.
— MAYA ANGELOU, in Claudia Tate (ed), *Black Women Writers at Work*, 1983

 *Taxes*

It has been said that one man's loophole is another man's livelihood. . . . It certainly is not fair, because the loophole-livelihood of those who are reaping undeserved benefits can be the economic noose of those who are paying more than they should.
— MILLICENT FENWICK, *Speaking Up*, 1982

Why does a slight tax increase cost you two hundred dollars and a substantial tax cut save you thirty cents?
— PEG BRACKEN, *I Didn't Come Here to Argue*, 1969

Tea

There's nothing like tea in the afternoon. When the British Empire collapses, historians will find that it had made but two invaluable contributions to civilization—this tea ritual and the detective novel.
— AYN RAND, *The Fountainhead,* 1943

Bernie made the kind of tea a mouse could stand on.
— LIZA CODY, *Dupe,* 1981

Teaching

I touch the future. I teach.
— CHRISTA MCAULIFFE, speech, August 1985, in *Time,* February 10, 1986

Teaching is practice in being real.
— NATALIE GOLDBERG, *Wild Mind,* 1990

I am teaching. It's kind of like having a love affair with a rhinoceros.
— ANNE SEXTON, in Linda Gray Sexton and Lois Ames (eds), *Anne Sexton: A Self-Portrait in Letters,* 1977

Teenagers

Teenagers travel in droves, packs, swarms. . . . To the librarian, they're a gaggle of geese. To the cook, they're a scourge of locusts. To department stores, they're a big beautiful exaltation of larks . . . all lovely and loose and jingly.
— BERNICE FITZ-GIBBON, director of advertising at Macy's, *New York Times,* June 6, 1960

(*See also* Adolescence, Childhood, Children, Daughters, Family, Fathers, Growing Up, Mothers, Mothers and Sons, Mothers-Daughters, Parenting, Youth)

Television

Television represents what happens to a medium when the artists have no power and the businessmen are in full, unquestioned control.

— PAULINE KAEL, *Reeling,* 1976

TV has opened many doors—mostly on refrigerators.

— MARY H. WALDRIP, in *Reader's Digest,* 1989

I finally figured out why soap operas are, and logically should be, so popular with generations of housebound women. They are the only place in our culture where grownup men take seriously all the things that grownup women have to deal with all day long.

— GLORIA STEINEM, *Outrageous Acts and Everyday Rebellions,* 1983

When television is bad, nothing is worse. When television is good, it's not much better. Why do you think it's called a medium?

— SUSAN OHANIAN, *Ask Ms. Class,* 1996

There is something spurious about the very term "a movie made for TV" because what you make for TV is a TV program.

— PAULINE KAEL, *Reeling,* 1976

There are days when any electrical appliance in the house, including the vacuum cleaner, seems to offer more entertainment possibilities than the TV set.

— HARRIET VAN HORNE, in *New York World-Telegram and Sun,* 1957

Theater

Failure in the theater is more dramatic and uglier than in any other form of writing. It costs so much, you feel so guilty.

— LILLIAN HELLMAN, in George Plimpton (ed), *Writers at Work,* 1967

I can never remember being afraid of an audience. If the audience could do better, they'd be up here on stage and I'd be out there watching them.

— ETHEL MERMAN, *Woman's Almanac*

People pay all that money to sit in a chair in the theater mainly because it is a respectable way to see and experience things they cannot see and experience in their own lives.

— ELIZABETH ASHLEY, *Actress,* 1978

It's as though some poor devil were to set out for a large dinner party with the knowledge that the following morning he would be hearing exactly what each of the other guests thought of him.

— CORNELIA OTIS SKINNER, on opening night reviews, *The Ape Is Me,* 1959

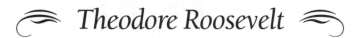

Theodore Roosevelt

My father always wanted to be the corpse at every funeral, the bride at every wedding and the baby at every christening.

— ALICE ROOSEVELT LONGWORTH, on President Theodore Roosevelt, in *Celebrity Register,* by Cleveland Amory and Earl Blackwell, 1963

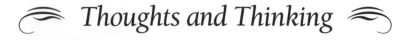

Thoughts and Thinking

My thoughts are like waffles—the first few don't look so good.
— MARILYN VOS SAVANT, in *Parade*, 1992

It is all right to say exactly what you think if you have learned to think exactly.
— MARCELENE COX, in *Ladies' Home Journal*, 1945

She nibbled away at her thought like a rabbit with a piece of lettuce.
— RAE FOLEY, *Death and Mr. Potter*, 1955

I can't see that she could have found anything nastier to say if she'd thought it out with both hands for a fortnight.
— DOROTHY L. SAYERS, *Busman's Honeymoon*, 1957

Borrowed thoughts, like borrowed money, only show the poverty of the borrower.
— LADY MARGUERITE BLESSINGTON, in R. R. Madden, *The Literary Life and Correspondence of the Countess of Blessington*, 1855

Time

All my possessions for a moment of time.
— ELIZABETH I, alleged last words, 1603

The insolence of time is like a blow in the face from an unseen enemy.
— MARGARET DELAND, *Sidney*, 1890

Fate carries its own clock.
— PEARL BAILEY, *The Raw Pearl*, 1968

It is so seldom in this world that things come just when they are wanted.
➤ MARGARET OLIPHANT, *The Perpetual Curate,* 1870

If we take care of the moments, the years will take care of themselves.
➤ MARIA EDGEWORTH, *Moral Tales,* 1801

Time was an accordion, all the air squeezed out of it as you grew older.
➤ HELEN HOOVEN SANTMYER, *And the Ladies of the Club,* 1984

(*See also* Age, Mature Love)

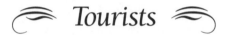 *Tourists*

Traveling is, and has always been, more popular than the traveler.
➤ AGNES REPPLIER, *Times and Tendencies,* 1931

Many Americans . . . dress for travel in cheap, comfortable, childish clothes, as if they were going to the zoo and would not be seen by anyone except the animals.
➤ ALISON LURIE, *The Language of Clothes,* 1981

One never feels such distaste for one's countrymen and countrywomen as when one meets them abroad.
➤ ROSE MACAULAY, *Crewe Train,* 1926

 *Travel*

The more I traveled the more I realized that fear makes strangers of people who would be friends.
➤ SHIRLEY MACLAINE, *Don't Fall Off the Mountain,* 1970

If I had my life to live over, I would have seen more of the world and enjoyed being somewhere else instead of staying home and worrying about things.

— ERMA BOMBECK column

Before one actually visits them, everyone tends to think of their favorite countries as one grand Disneyland filled with national monuments and historical treasures conveniently laid out for easy viewing, when what they really are filled with, of course, is people going to work, laundromats and places to buy rat poison.

— BETTE MIDLER, *A View From a Broad,* 1980

Men travel faster now, but I do not know if they go to better things.

— WILLA CATHER, *Death Comes for the Archbishop,* 1927

I think that to get under the surface and really appreciate the beauty of any country, one has to go there poor.

— GRACE MOORE, *You're Only Human Once,* 1944

Trees

Trees are nearly as important as men, and much better behaved.

— WINIFRED HOLTBY, in *Letters to a Friend,* 1937

I have watched the trees when they pray, and I've watched them shout and sometimes they give thanks slowly and quietly.

— BESSIE HARVEY, in *Black Art—Ancestral Legacy,* 1989

When I stepped away from the white pine, I had the definite feeling that we had exchanged some form of life energy. . . . Clearly white pines and I are on the same wavelength. What I give back to the trees I cannot imagine. I hope they receive something, because trees are among my closest friends.

— ANNE LABASTILLE, *Woodswoman,* 1976

Everybody who's anybody longs to be a tree—
or ride one, hair blown to froth.
That's why horses were invented
— RITA DOVE, *Grace Notes*, 1989

Trouble

The blow you can't see coming is the one that knocks you out.
— JOYCE CAROL OATES, *Raven's Wing*, 1985

Women like to sit down with trouble as if it were knitting.
— ELLEN GLASGOW, *The Sheltered Life*, 1932

What fresh hell is this?
— DOROTHY PARKER, on the ringing of a doorbell or telephone,
in Marion Meade, *Dorothy Parker: What Fresh Hell Is This?*
1988

Flowers grow
out of the dark
moments
— CORITA KENT, *Moments*, 1982

Trust

He who has trusted where he ought not will surely mistrust where
he ought not.
— MARIE VON EBNER-ESCHENBACH, *Aphorisms*, 1893

How can the people trust the harvest unless they see it sown?
— MARY RENAULT, *The King Must Die*, 1958

How desperately we wish to maintain our trust in those we love! In the face of everything, we try to find reasons to trust. Because losing faith is worse than falling out of love.

— SONIA JOHNSON, *From Housewife to Heretic,* 1981

Truth

Truth is a rough, honest, helter-skelter terrier, that none like to see brought into their drawing-rooms.

— OUIDA, *Wisdom, Wit and Pathos,* 1884

You cannot weave truth on a loom of lies.

— SUZETTE HADEN ELGIN, *Native Tongue,* 1984

Truth lies at the bottom of a well. Were I to look into that well and report to you what I saw, I would be describing my own image, my own truth.

— BONNIE JONES REYNOLDS, *The Truth About Unicorns,* 1973

Truth has divine properties, and the ability to see it is a gift that's given, not acquired.

— KATHERINE NEVILLE, *A Calculated Risk,* 1992

Every new truth begins in a shocking heresy.

— MARGARET DELAND, *The Keys,* 1924

I have somewhere suggested, I think, that when your fancy is taken by a young man of slender figure and pleasing profile, you should not disclose at too early a stage the true nature of your interest.

— SARAH CAUDWELL, *The Shortest Way to Hades,* 1984

Understanding

You always admire what you do not understand.

ELEANOR ROOSEVELT, in *Meeet the Press*, NBC broadcast, September 16,
    1956

When we find that we are not liked, we assert that we are not
understood; when probably the dislike we have excited proceeds
from our being too fully comprehended.

— COUNTESS OF BLESSINGTON, *Desultory Thoughts and Reflections*,
    1839

Nothing's easier than believing we understand experiences we've
never had.

— GWEN BRISTOW, *Tomorrow Is Forever*, 1943

We
do not admire what
we cannot understand.

— MARIANNE MOORE, *Selected Poems*, 1935

United States

America was founded on a genocide, on the unquestioned assump-
tion of the right of white Europeans to exterminate a resident,
technologically backward, colored population in order to take over
the continent.

— SUSAN SONTAG, *Styles of Radical Will*, 1966

The United States is an enormous frosted cupcake in the middle of
millions of starving people.

— GLORIA STEINEM, *Moving Beyond Words*, 1994

It is a spiritually impoverished nation that permits infants and children to be the poorest Americans.

➤ MARIAN WRIGHT EDELMAN, *The Measure of Our Success,* 1992

American society is very like a fish society. . . . Among certain species of fish, the only thing which determines order of dominance is length of time in the fishbowl. The oldest resident picks on the newest resident, and if the newest resident is removed to a new bowl, he as oldest resident will pick on the newcomers.

➤ MARGARET MEAD, *And Keep Your Powder Dry,* 1942

I don't measure America by its achievement, but by its potential.

➤ SHIRLEY CHISHOLM, *Unbought and Unbossed,* 1970

They are noisy and talkative but very reserved, self-conscious and a little hypocritical, but they burn more boats and throw their bonnets over more windmills than any people on earth.

➤ NANCY HOYT, *Roundabout,* 1926

Every American carries in his bloodstream the heritage of the malcontent and the dreamer.

➤ DOROTHY FULDHEIM, *A Thousand Friends,* 1974

In the United States there is more space where nobody is than where anybody is. That is what makes America what it is.

➤ GERTRUDE STEIN, *The Geographical History of America,* 1936

The melting pot's . . . purpose is to produce that "All-American" product. And that product is certainly not dark-skinned, does not speak American Sign Language or with an "ethnic accent," is not poor, is certainly not lesbian or gay, and is not old.

➤ PAULA ROSS, in Valerie Miner and Helen Longino (eds), *Competition,* 1987

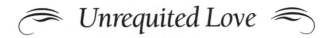

Unrequited Love

Love clamors far more incessantly and passionately at a closed gate than an open one!

— MARIE CORELLI, *The Master Christian*, 1900

To love somebody
Who doesn't love you
Is like going to a temple
And worshipping the behind
Of a wooden statue
Of a hungry devil.

— LADY KASA (8th century), in Joanna Bankier and Deirdre Lash-gari (eds), *Women Poets of the World*, 1983

(*See also* Affairs, Dating, Heart, Love Versus Hate)

Unwed Mothers

it was good for the virgin Mary
it's good enough for me

— NIKKI GIOVANNI, "Poem for Unwed Mothers," *Re-Creation*, 1970

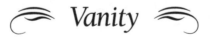

Vanity

There is scarcely any fault in another which offends us more than vanity, though perhaps there is none that really injures us so little.

— HANNAH MORE, *Practical Piety*, 1811

We are so vain that we even care for the opinion of those we don't care for.

— MARIE VON EBNER-ESCHENBACH, *Aphorisms*, 1905

Vice

The vices of the rich and great are mistaken for error; and those of the poor and lowly, for crimes.
> ━ LADY MARGUERITE BLESSINGTON, *Desultory Thoughts and Reflections,* 1839

Victory

More people are ruined by victory, I imagine, than by defeat.
> ━ ELEANOR ROOSEVELT, *My Days,* 1938

If you live long enough, you'll see that every victory turns into a defeat.
> ━ SIMONE DE BEAUVOIR, *All Men Are Mortal,* 1946

Virginity

Sometimes when I look at all my children, I say to myself, "Lillian, you should have stayed a virgin."
> ━ LILLIAN CARTER, comment to 1980 Democratic Convention that nominated her son for a second term as president, quoted in *Newsweek,* December 29, 1980

War

War settles nothing. To win a war is as disastrous as to lose one.
> ━ AGATHA CHRISTIE, *An Autobiography,* 1977

Two things are always the same: the dance, and war.
— GERTRUDE STEIN, *Everybody's Autobiography,* 1937

Dead battles, like dead generals, hold the military mind in their dead grip.
— BARBARA TUCHMAN, *The Guns of August,* 1962

As a woman I can't go to war, and I refuse to send anyone else.
— JEANETTE RANKIN, in Hannah Josephson, *Lady in Congress,* 1974

War is, undoubtedly, hell, but there is no earthly reason why it has to start so early in the morning.
— FRAN LEBOWITZ, *Social Studies,* 1981

It is true we have won all our wars, but we have paid for them. We don't want victories anymore.
— GOLD MEIR, *Life,* October 3, 1969

(*See also* Enemies)

Washington, D.C.

In Washington it is an honor to be disgraced. By that I mean you have to have been somebody to fall.
— MEG GREENFIELD, in *Newsweek,* 1986

Washington is a town where more people probably contemplate writing a book than finish reading one.
— ANN GERACIMOS, *Washington Times,* March 29, 1989

Too small to be a state but too large to be an asylum for the mentally deranged.
— ANNE M. BURFORD, in *The Washington Post,* 1984

Washington knows that it is not safe to kick people who are down until you find out what their next stop will be.

— JUDITH MARTIN, *Style and Substance,* 1986

If there are more than two people [in Washington] together . . . one of them is climbing.

— SALLY QUINN, *We're Going to Make You a Star,* 1975

 *Wealth*

A large income is the best recipe for happiness I ever heard of.

— JANE AUSTEN, in *The Book of Success,* edited by Richard Shea, 1993

To be content with little is difficult; to be content with much, impossible.

— MARIE VON EBNER-ESCHENBACH, *Aphorisms,* 1893

Just because you're rich doesn't mean you're not cheap.

— CATHY SEIBEL, on the prosecution of hotel owner Leona Helmsley, in *The New York Times,* August 24, 1989

 *Weddings*

The organ pealed forth. . . . In every heart began to spring that exquisite hope, seldom if ever realized, that the bride will have had a fit, or eloped with someone else.

— ANGELA THIRKELL, *Cheerfulness Breaks In,* 1941

O how short a time does it take to put an eternal end to a woman's liberty!

— FANNY BURNEY, after attending a wedding (1768), in Annie Raine Ellis (ed), *The Early Diary of Frances Burney,* 1889

Weight

The wild emaciated look appeals to some women, though not to many men, who are seldom seen pinning up a *Vogue* illustration in a machine shop.

— PEG BRACKEN, appendix to the *I Hate to Cook Book*, 1966

When women are excited about a date, they go immediately on a diet, because all women know they are hideously obese.

— CYNTHIA HEIMEL, *Get Your Tongue Out of My Mouth, I'm Kissing You Goodbye!* 1993

Whites

"Native" always means people who belong somewhere else, because they had once belonged somewhere. That shows that the white race does not really think they belong anywhere, because they think of everybody else as native.

— GERTRUDE STEIN, *Everybody's Autobiography*, 1937

The white race is the cancer of human history. It is the white race, and it alone—its ideologies and inventions—which eradicates autonomous civilizations where it spreads.

— SUSAN SONTAG, in *Partisan Review*, winter 1967

How in the hell could God take the black earth and make himself a white man out of it?

— LOUISE MERIWETHER, *Daddy Was a Number Runner*, 1970

Most of the time when "universal" is used, it's just a euphemism for "white"; white themes, white significance, white culture.

— MERLE WOO, in Cherrie Moraga and Gloria Anzaldua (eds), *This Bridge Called My Back*, 1983

Wildlife

Probably we never fully credit the interdependence of wild creatures, and their cognizance of the affairs of their own kind.
— MARY AUSTIN, *The Land of Little Rain,* 1904

One of the things I like best about animals in the wild is that they're always off on some errand. They have appointments to keep. It's only we humans who wonder what we're here for.
— DIANE ACKERMAN, *The Moon by Whale Light,* 1991

Captivity, no matter how kind, is always cruel.
— JOAN WARD HARRIS, **Creature Comforts,** 1979

If you look close . . . you can see that the wild critters have "No Trespassing" tacked up on every pine tree.
— MARGUERITE HENRY, *Misty of Chincoteague,* 1947

Wine

Great people talk about ideas, average people talk about things, small people talk about wine.
— FRAN LEBOWITZ, *Social Studies,* 1981

Wine is earth's answer to the sun.
— MARGARET FULLER, in Lydia Maria Child, *Letters From New York,* 1845

Winning

Whoever said, "It's not whether you win or lose that counts" probably lost.
— MARTINA NAVRATILOVA, in Roz Warren (ed), *Glibquips*, 1994

Successful competitors want to win. Head cases want to win at all costs.
— NANCY LOPEZ, in *The Golfer's Book of Wisdom*, edited by Criswell Freeman, 1995

The one who cared the most wins. That's how I knew I'd end up with everyone else waving the white flags and not me. That's how I knew I'd be the last person standing when it was all over. I cared the most.
— ROSEANNE ARNOLD, *My Lives*, 1994

Winter

Winter lies too long in country towns; hangs on until it is stale and shabby, old and sullen.
— WILLA CATHER, *My Ántonia*, 1918

Winter could drop down out of a clear sky, sharp as an icicle, and without a sound, pierce your heart.
— JESSAMYN WEST, *The Massacre at Fall Creek*, 1975

Wives

While I was ironing one evening, it suddenly occurred to me that I, too, would like to have a wife. My God, who wouldn't want a wife?
— JUDY SYFERS, *Ms*, 1972

Wife and servant are the same
But only differ in the name
— LADY MARY CHUDLEIGH, *Poems on Several Occasions,* 1773

 *Women*

Handle with care: women, glass and love.
— SWEDISH PROVERB

I was tired of being a woman,
tired of the spoons and the pots,
tired of my mouth and my breasts,
tired of the cosmetics and the silks . . .
I was tired of the gender of things.
— ANNE SEXTON, *Live or Die,* 1967

Women never have young minds. They are born three thousand years old.
— SHELAGH DELANEY, *A Taste of Honey,* 1957

The Old Testament makes woman a mere afterthought in creation; the author of evil; cursed in her maternity; a subject in marriage; and all female life, animal and human, unclean.
— ELIZABETH CADY STANTON, *The Woman's Bible,* 1898

The great and almost only comfort about being a woman is that one can always pretend to be more stupid than one is, and no one is surprised.
— DAME FREYA MADELEINE STARK, *The Valley of the Assassins,* 1934

Woman is shut up in a kitchen or in a boudoir, and astonishment is expressed that her horizon is limited. Her wings are clipped, and it is found deplorable that she cannot fly.
— SIMONE DE BEAUVOIR, *The Second Sex,* 1949

Too many women in too many countries speak the same language—silence.

— Anasuya Sengupta, "Silence," news item, 1995

Well-behaved women rarely make history.

— Laurel Thatcher Ulrich, in Kay Mills, *From Pocahontas to Power Suits,* 1995

Why have women passion, intellect, moral activity—these three—and a place in society where no one of the three can be exercised?

— Florence Nightingale, *Suggestions for Thought to Searchers after Religious Truth,* 1859; published as an appendix in Ray Strachey, *The Cause: A Short History of the Women's Movement in Great Britain,* 1928

A woman is a foreign land,
Of which, though there he settle young,
A man will ne'er quite understand
The customs, politics, and tongue

— Coventry Patmore, *Angel in the House,* 1856

We are becoming the men we wanted to marry.

— Gloria Steinem, *Ms,* 1982

I think women need kindness more than love.

— Alice Childress, "Alice Childress," in *Interviews with Contemporary Women Playwrights,* by Kathleen Betsko and Rachel Koenig, 1987

Being a woman is worse than being a farmer—There is so much harvesting and crop spraying to be done: legs to be waxed, underarms shaved, eyebrows plucked, feet pumiced, skin exfoliated and moisturized, spots cleansed, roots dyed, eyelashes tinted, nails filed, cellulite massaged, stomach muscles exercised . . . is it any wonder girls have no confidence?

— Helen Fielding, *Bridget Jones's Diary,* 1996

A woman who is loved always has success.

— VICKI BAUM, *Grand Hotel*, 1929

(*See also* Feminism, Housework, Women and Education, Women's Rights, Working Women)

Women and Education

If neither governesses or mothers know, how can they teach? So long as education is not provided for them, how can it be provided by them?

— SARAH EMILY DAVIES (1860–1908), *Thoughts on Some Questions Relating to Women*

(*See also* Housework, Mothers, Women, Women's Rights, Women Versus Men, Working Women)

Women's Rights

A backlash against women's rights is nothing new. Indeed it's a recurring phenomenon: it returns every time women begin to make some headway towards equality, a seemingly inevitable early frost to the brief flowerings of feminism.

— SUSAN FALUDI, *Backlash*, 1992

This mad, wicked folly of "Women's Rights" with all its attendant horrors, on which her poor sex is bent, forgetting every sense of womanly feeling and propriety. Lady Amberley ought to get a good whipping.

— QUEEN VICTORIA, in letter to Sir Theodore Martin about the feminist Lady Amberley (Bertrand Russell's mother), March 29, 1870

The history of men's opposition to women's emancipation is more interesting perhaps than the story of that emancipation itself.

— VIRGINIA WOOLF, *A Room of One's Own,* 1929

Men have always got so many "good reasons" for keeping their privileges. If we had left it to the men, toilets would have been the greatest obstacle to human progress. Toilets were always the reason women couldn't become engineers, or pilots, or even members of parliament. They didn't have women's toilets.

— HAZEL HUNKINS HALLINAN, in Dale Spender, *There's Always Been a Woman's Movement,* 1983

If women understand by emancipation the adoption of the masculine role then we are lost indeed.

— GERMAINE GREER, *The Female Eunuch,* 1970

Look at me! Look at my arm! I have plowed, and planted, and gathered into barns, and no man could head me—and aren't I a woman? I could work as much and eat as much as a man (when I could get it) and bear the lash as well—and aren't I a woman? I have borne 13 children and seen 'em most all sold off into slavery, and when I cried out with a mother's grief, none but Jesus heard— and aren't I a woman?

— SOJOURNER TRUTH, 1851 Women's Right Convention, Akron, Ohio, quoted in *Narrative of Sojourner Truth,* 1875

The men are much alarmed by certain speculations about women; and well they may be, for when the horse and ass begin to think and argue, adieu to riding and driving.

— ADELAIDE ANNE PROCTER, letter to Anna Jameson, 1838, in Geraldine Macpherson, *Memoirs of the Life of Anna Jameson,* 1878

I'm furious about the Women's Liberationists. They keep getting up on soapboxes and proclaiming that women are brighter than men. That's true, but it should be kept very quiet or it ruins the whole racket.

— ANITA LOOS, in *London Observer,* December 30, 1973

The sadness of the women's movement is that they don't allow the necessity of love. See, I don't personally trust any revolution where love is not allowed.

— MAYA ANGELOU, May 14, 1975, interview in *California Living,* collected in *Conversations with Maya Angelou,* 1989

(*See also* Housework, Mothers, Women, Women and Education, Women Versus Men, Working Women)

Women Versus Men

Men are like the earth and we are the moon; we turn always one side to them, and they think there is no other, because they don't see it—but there is.

— OLIVE EMILY SCHREINER, *The Story of an African Farm,* 1883

If a woman drinks the last glass of apple juice in the refrigerator, she'll make more apple juice. If a man drinks the last glass of apple juice, he'll just put back the empty container.

— RITA RUDNER, *First,* 1993

The basic discovery about any people is the discovery of the relationship between its men and women.

— PEARL S. BUCK, *Of Men and Women,* 1941

What would happen if . . . men could menstruate and women could not? Clearly, menstruation would become an enviable, boastworthy, masculine event: Men would brag about how long and how much. Young boys would talk about it as the envied beginning of manhood. Generals, right-wing politicians, and religious fundamentalists would cite . . . "mens-truation" as proof that only men could serve God and country in combat. If men could menstruate, the power justifications would go on and on. If we let them.

— GLORIA STEINEM, collected in *Outrageous Acts and Everyday Rebellions,* 1983

Women are more quiet. They don't feel called to mount a barrel and harangue by the hour every time they imagine they have produced an idea.

— ANNA JULIA COOPER, *A Voice in the South*, 1892

Men are the Brahmin, women the Pariahs, under our existing civilization.

— ELIZABETH CADY STANTON, *The History of Woman Suffrage*, 1881

In politics, if you want anything said, ask a man. If you want anything done, ask a woman.

— MARGARET THATCHER, speech, 1965, quoted in *People*, September 15, 1975

If a woman gets nervous, she'll eat or go shopping. A man will attack a country—it's a whole other way of thinking.

— ELAYNE BOOSLER, in Gloria Kaufman, *In Stitches*, 1991

A man would never get the notion of writing a book on the peculiar situation of the human male.

— SIMONE DE BEAUVOIR, *The Second Sex*, 1953

Women want mediocre men, and men are working hard to be as mediocre as possible.

— MARGARET MEAD, *Quote*, May 15, 1958

To be happy with a man you must understand him a lot and love him a little. To be happy with a woman you must love her a lot and not try to understand her at all.

— HELEN ROWLAND, *A Guide to Men*, 1922

Men look *at* themselves in a mirror. Women look *for* themselves.

— ELISSA MELAMED, *Mirror, Mirror: The Terror of Not Being Young*, 1983

The mulish short-sightedness of most Englishmen is such that they do not give women flowers, because they themselves can see no point to it—an attitude about as logical as refusing to bait a hook with a worm because you yourself are no worm-eater.

— KATHERINE WHITEHORN, *Roundabout,* 1962

I require only three things of a man:
He must be handsome, ruthless and stupid.

— DOROTHY PARKER, *You Might As Well Live,* 1971

A man falls in love through his eyes, a woman through her imagination, and then they both speak of it as an affair of "the heart."

— HELEN ROWLAND, *A Guide to Men,* 1922

A man in the house is worth two in the street.

— MAE WEST, in *Belle of the Nineties,* 1934

Women are not men's equals in anything except responsibility. We are not their inferiors, either, or even their superiors. We are quite simply different races.

— PHYLLIS MCGINLEY, *The Province of the Heart,* 1959

Women speak because they wish to speak, whereas a man speaks only when driven to speech by something outside himself—like, for instance, he can't find any clean socks.

— JEAN KERR, *The Snake Has All the Lines,* 1960

We all marry strangers. All men are strangers to all women.

— MARY HEATON VORSE, "The Pink Fence," in *McCall's,* 1920

(*See also* Housework, Men, Mothers, Women, Women and Education, Women's Rights, Working Women)

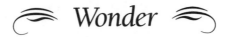 *Wonder*

For the first time in her life she thought, might the same wonders never come again? Was each wonder original and alone like the falling star, and when it fell, did it bury itself beyond where you hunted it?
— EUDORA WELTY, *The Wide Net,* 1943

Wonder is music heard in the heart.
— ROSEMARY DOBSON, *Selected Poems,* 1973

If a child is to keep alive his inborn sense of wonder, he needs the companionship of at least one adult who can share it, rediscovering with him the joy, excitement and mystery of the world we live in.
— RACHEL CARSON, *The Sense of Wonder,* 1965

 *Words*

Give the people a new word and they think they have a new fact.
— WILLA CATHER, "On Writing," *Four Letters: Escapism,* 1936

The true call of the desert, of the mountains, or the sea, is their silence—free of the networks of dead speech.
— DAME FREYA MADELEINE STARK, *Perseus in the Wind,* 1948

Words, like children, have the power to make dance the dullest beanbag of a heart.
— PEGGY NOONAN, *What I Saw at the Revolution,* 1990

There's a hell of a distance between wise-cracking and wit. Wit has truth in it; wise-cracking is simply calisthenics with words.
— DOROTHY PARKER, in the *Paris Review,* summer 1956

Work

One never notices what has been done; one can only see what remains to be done.

— MARIE CURIE, letter, 1894

The person who knows "how" will always have a job. The person who knows "why" will always be his boss.

— DIANE SILVERS RAVITCH, speech at Reed College commencement, reported in *Time*, June 17, 1985

It is not hard work that is dreary; it is superficial work.

— EDITH HAMILTON in Doris Fielding Reid, *Edith Hamilton*, 1967

That society exists to frustrate the individual may be seen from its attitude to work. It is only morally acceptable if you don't want to do it. If you do want to, it becomes a personal pleasure.

— CELIA GREEN, *The Decline and Fall of Science*, 1976

Working Women

Being a housewife and a mother is the biggest job in the world, but if it doesn't interest you, don't do it. It didn't interest me, so I didn't do it. Anyway, I would have made a terrible parent. The first time my child didn't do what I wanted, I'd kill him.

— KATHARINE HEPBURN, in Liz Smith, *The Mother Book* (1978)

At work, you think of the children you have left at home. At home, you think of the work you've left unfinished. Such a struggle is unleashed within yourself. Your heart is rent.

— GOLDA MEIR, in *L'Europeo*, by Oriana Fallaci, 1973

Hard labor: A redundancy, like "working mother."

— JOYCE ARMOR, *The Dictionary According to Mommy,* 1990

I think we're seeing in working mothers a change from "Thank God It's Friday" to "Thank God It's Monday." If any working mother has not experienced that feeling, her children are not adolescent.

— ANN DIEHL, *Vogue,* January 1985

You think, dear Johannes, that because I occasionally lay something aside I am giving too many concerts. But think of my responsibilities—seven children still dependent on me, five who have yet to be educated.

— CLARA SCHUMANN, after Robert Schumann's death (1861), in Berthold Litzmann (ed), *Letters of Clara Schumann and Johannes Brahms,* vol 1, 1927

Being asked to decide between your passion for work and your passion for children was like being asked by your doctor whether you preferred him to remove your brain or your heart.

— MARY KAY BLAKELY, *American Mom,* 1994

Why not have your first baby at 60, when your husband is already dead and your career is over? Then you can really devote yourself to it.

— FRAN LEBOWITZ, in *Redbook,* 1990

Why was I born beneath two curses,
To bear children and to write verses?
Either one fecundity
Were heavy enough destiny.
But all my life is penalty
From the two sides of me.

— ANNA WICKHAM, "New Eve" (1915), in R. D. Smith (ed), *The Writings of Anna Wickham,* 1984

The test for whether or not you can hold a job should not be the arrangement of your chromosomes
— BELLA ABZUG, in *Bella!* by Mel Ziegler, 1972

The more women are paid, the less eager they are to marry.
— SUSAN FALUDI, *Backlash*, 1992

World

I was in love with the whole world and all that lived in its rainy arms.
— LOUISE ERDRICH, *Love Medicine*, 1984

Worry

While most of the things you've worried about have never happened, it's a different story with the things you haven't worried about. They are the ones that happen.
— RUTH RENDELL, *Talking to Strange Men*, 1987

'Tain't worthwhile to wear a day all out before it comes.
— SARAH ORNE JEWETT, *The Country of the Pointed Firs*, 1896

Worry is like racing the engine of an automobile without letting in the clutch.
— CORRIE TEN BOOM, *Don't Wrestle, Just Nestle*, 1978

Writers

I didn't set out to be a feminist writer. I just look at the sheep out of the window and watch their behavior.
— FAY WELDON, in *The Observer*, 1989

We write because we love the world, and why not finally carry that secret out with our bodies into the living rooms and porches, backyards and grocery stores? Let the whole thing flower: the poem and the person writing the poem. And let us always be kind to this world.

— NATALIE GOLDBERG, *Writing Down the Bones,* 1993

Most of the basic material a writer works with is acquired before the age of 15.

— WILLA CATHER, *Willa Cather,* 1930

I've never met a writer who wanted to be anything else.

— NATALIE GOLDBERG, *Wild Mind,* 1990

Writing

Writing and money appear to be mutually exclusive.

— RITA MAE BROWN, *Starting From Scratch,* 1988

Every book is like a purge; at the end of it, one is empty . . . like a dry shell on the beach, waiting for the tide to come in again.

— DAME DAPHNE DU MAURIER, in *Ladies' Home Journal,* November 1956

I think if you had ever written a book you were absolutely pleased with, you'd never write another. The same probably goes for children.

— FAY WELDON, in the *Guardian,* November 28, 1991

Writing is elemental. Once you have tasted its essential life, you cannot turn from it without some deep denial and depression. It would be like turning from water.

— NATALIE GOLDBERG, *Wild Mind,* 1990

I believe one writes because one has to create a world in which one can live.

— ANAÏS NIN, *The Diary of Anaïs Nin,* 1974

Youth

Why is youth so short and age so long?

— OUIDA (Marie Louise de la Ramée), *Pipistrello,* 1880

Why, I wonder, do people who at one time or another have all been young themselves, and who ought therefore to know better, generalize so suavely and so mendaciously about the golden hours of youth—that period of life when every sorrow seems permanent, and every setback insuperable?

— VERA BRITTAIN, *Testament of Youth,* 1933

Young folks don't want you to understand 'em. You've got no more right to understand them than you have to play their games or wear their clothes. They belong to themselves.

— EDNA FERBER, *Great Son,* 1944

As long as you can still be disappointed, you are still young.

— SARAH CHURCHILL, in *The Observer,* 1981

I've always believed in the adage that the secret of eternal youth is arrested development.

— ALICE ROOSEVELT LONGWORTH, *Mrs. L.: Conversations with Alice Roosevelt Longworth,* 1981

If youth did not matter so much to itself, it would never have the heart to go on.

— WILLA CATHER, *The Song of the Lark,* 1915

That's what being young is all about. You have the courage and the daring to think that you can make a difference. You're not prone to measure your energies in time.

— RUBY DEE, in Brian Lanker, *I Dream a World,* 1989

Index